The Acts of the Apostles

Study Hour
Commentaries

The Acts of the Apostles

Introduction and Notes by
W. GRAHAM SCROGGIE
D.D. (EDIN.)

LONDON
PICKERING & INGLIS LTD.

PICKERING & INGLIS LTD

ISBN 0 7208 0379 9
Cat. No. 01/0128

THE ACTS OF THE APOSTLES

Reprinted by special arrangement with Pickering & Inglis, Ltd.

First Zondervan printing   1976

Library of Congress Cataloging in Publication Data
Bible.   N.T. Acts.   English.   1976.
    The Acts of the Apostles.
    Reprint of the 1931 ed. published by Marshall, Morgan
& Scott, London, in series: The Study hour series.
    Bibliography: p.
    1.   Bible.   N.T.   Acts—Commentaries.   I. Scroggie,
William Graham, 1877-1958.   II. Title.   III. Series:
The Study hour series.
BS2623.S38   1976   226'.6'066   75-38802

Printed in the United States of America

INTRODUCTION

Charles Reade says that the *Book of the Acts* is one of the most graphic pieces of writing in all literature, and certainly it is one of the most important, for it is " the sole remaining historical work which deals with the beginnings of Church history."

The Book never had any· one title which commanded general acceptance, in some manuscripts being called " Acts," and in others " The Acts," " Acts of Apostles," " Acts of the Apostles," " The Acts of the Apostles." It is now commonly known by the last of these, although it is not an account of the doings of all the Apostles, but, in the main, of two of them only, nor is it a record of all the acts of these two. A negro convert has called it, not unsuitably, " Words about Deeds." Perhaps the most comprehensive title we could give to it would be " *The Acts of the Holy Spirit through Apostles and others, during the first generation of the history of the Christian Church.*"

AUTHORSHIP

From earliest days tradition has ascribed to Luke the authorship of this Book, and there is no reason to call that tradition into question. We may summarize the evidence for the Lukan authorship as follows : (1) The Third Gospel and the Acts are clearly from the same hand, for the same style, language and method characterize them both. (2) The author was a medical man, for in his narrative he uses a number of medical terms in a technical sense. A valuable and interesting book on this subject is, *The Medical Language of St. Luke*, by Hobart. (3) The author of the Acts was one of Paul's companions. This is shown in what is called the " We " sections of the Book, xvi. 10–17, xx. 5–15, xxi. 1–18, xxvii. 1–xxviii. 16. Whoever the author was, he joined Paul at Troas, and went with him to Philippi (xvi. 8–12), and he appears to have remained there until Paul returned in his third

5

missionary journey (xx. 5, 6). Ramsay thinks that the "*man of Macedonia*," whom Paul saw and heard in the vision at Troas, was Luke (*St. Paul*, pp. 202, 203), and it has been conjectured that he and Paul may have met in student days when Luke studied as a medical student in the university of Tarsus (Knowling, *Expositor's Greek Testament*). If this were so, Paul, because of the condition of his health, may have sought out Luke that he might have the benefit of his professional skill. (4) The fact that Luke's name does not occur in the Acts. If it be thought a mere conjecture that Luke should be read into the " We " of the above sections, the fact that his name does not occur in this Book must be accounted for. We know that he was one of Paul's companions, much beloved by him, and that he stood by him in days of darkness and danger (Philemon 24, Col. iv. 14, 2 Tim. iv. 11). Is it likely, then, that any one else writing this record would have failed to mention him ? But if Luke himself is the author, the suppression of his name is easily understood, as is the suppression of John's name in the Fourth Gospel. (5) The author of the Acts was with Paul at Rome (xxvii. 1–xxviii. 16), and Luke was with him there at that time (2 Tim. iv. 11). (6) An author writing this Book at a late date would certainly have used Paul's Epistles as sources for his work, for they are " the most weighty documents for the history which he professes to describe," but the Acts is written independently of them, and, as Knowling says, " it cannot be said that any one letter in particular is employed by the writer." But if Luke is the author, this silence cannot surprise us, for his knowledge would not need to be obtained from the Apostle's letters. All these considerations make it practically certain that the author of the Acts was " *Luke the beloved physician.*"

DATE

Three views have been held on this point. First, that the Acts was written early in the second century.

This view is really untenable on a number of grounds, and, probably, would never have been held except for the supposition that the author made use of the writings of Josephus. Second, that the Book was written between A.D. 70 and 90, and, probably, about A.D. 80. This view is based on the assumption that Luke's Gospel was written after the destruction of Jerusalem (A.D. 70), ch. xxi. 20 ff., being pointed to as evidence. But if the Acts had been written within ten or twelve years after that tragic event, surely some mention would have been made of it! Third, that the Book was written in the year A.D. 63. The grounds for this view are that " after the burning of Rome (A.D. 64), and the destruction of Jerusalem, the attitude maintained in the Book towards Romans and Jews would have been very difficult unless the date was a long time afterward " (A. T. Robertson). This date (A.D. 63) best suits all the facts and requirements.

UNITY

If the Lukan authorship of the Acts be granted, it will scarcely be necessary to discuss its unity, for, in that case, it could not be the work of " a number of writers who have gradually compiled the book by collecting and piecing together scraps of other books, and by altering or cutting out such passages in the same as seemed inconsistent with their particular opinions." It is practically certain that the author of the " We " sections is also the author of the rest of the Book, and that he was controlled by a definite object in writing. The idea of a number of redactors or editors working over a number of sources can scarcely be taken seriously. The impression left upon one from reading the Book is that it is a story coherent and progressive, and a detailed study of it confirms this impression.

SOURCES

But when we speak of the unity of the Acts, we do not mean that the author had no recourse to

7

sources of information, oral or written. In the "We" sections such were not necessary, as the writer was a witness of what he relates, but this is not the case in the other parts of the Book. For information concerning events of which Luke was not an eye-witness, he must, of course, have been dependent on others, and his method of investigation is stated in his Gospel (i. 1-4). The question is, therefore, not "Did Luke use sources?" but, "What sources did he use?" A detailed consideration of this matter is outside the scope of this Series, and those who would know what has been said on the subject are referred to Knowling on the Acts, *Expositor's Greek Testament*, pp. 17-33, or to a good Bible Dictionary, but very briefly we would indicate the line of investigation. As already said, chapters xvi. 10-17, xx. 5-15, xxi, 1-18, xxvii. 1–xxviii. 16, are accounted for, Luke being an eye-witness. For the remainder of the record Luke was dependent on persons who had knowledge of the events he records. First and foremost of these, of course, was Paul. Luke was much with him, and during times of enforced inactivity, as at Caesarea, and Malta, and Rome, and, as Zahn says, nothing is more natural than that the great missionary should have communicated to his beloved friend the records of his work and experience in great heathen centres of commercial or intellectual life, like Corinth, Ephesus, Athens. This would account for everything in the Acts from chapter xiii.

What is related in chapter xii. he might well have got from Mark, to whose house Peter went after his release from prison, and who was with Luke in Rome (Cor. iv. 10). Cornelius, who lived at Caesarea (x. 1) could have given Luke the information for the major part of chapters ix.-xi., for Luke was at Caesara with Paul. The details of chapters vi.-vii. he could have got from Paul, who witnessed the martyrdom of Stephen, and of chapter viii. from Philip, who lived at Caesarea, and was one of the seven (vi. 5, xxi. 8). This accounts for chapters vi-xxviii. of the Acts, in a highly reasonable and probable way. The sources of chapters i.-v. are not so clear, but Peter, Barnabas, and Philip, who enter into this history, and who were known to Luke, might well have supplied him with the details which he records. The Acts, however, is not a collection of reports from various sources, but the work of one " thoroughly independent in style," and who " assimilated his materials like a true historian."—(A. T. Robertson).

CHRONOLOGY

The Chronology of the Acts is a vexed question for which, in detail, the reader must consult Bengel, Wendt, Zahn, Ramsay, Harnack, Holtzmann, Turner, and others ; but the following will serve as an approximate working scheme on important events :—

A.D. 30. Death of Jesus.
  35. Conversion of Paul. (ix.)
  44. Death of James, son of Zebedee. (xii.)
 45-51. First missionary journey. (xiii.-xiv.)
  51. Conference at Jerusalem. (xv.)
 51-54. Second missionary journey. (xvi.-xviii.)
 54-58. Third missionary journey. (xviii.-xxi.)
  58. Paul's arrest in Jerusalem. (xxi.)
 58-60. Caesarean imprisonment. (xxiv.-xxvi.)
 61-63. First Roman imprisonment. (xxviii.)

Into any scheme must be worked the various references in the Acts to Paul's sojourn in various places, for example, his three years in Arabia and Damascus (Gal. i. 18), his sojourn with Barnabas at Antioch for " *a whole year* " (xi. 26), his stay at Antioch for a " *long time* " upon the return from the first missionary journey (xiv. 26-28), the Jerusalem Conference (xv.), the waiting at Athens (xvii. 16), the eighteen months at Corinth (xviii. 11), the interval between the second and third missionary journeys, which is spoken of as " *some time* " (xviii. 22, 23), the three years in Ephesus (xix. 10, xx. 31), the three months in Corinth (xx. 3), the " *many days* " at Caesarea (xxi. 10), the sojourn at Jerusalem (xxi. 15–xxiii. 22), the two years in Caesarea (xxiii. 23–xxvi. 32, cf. xxiv. 27), the journey to Malta (xxvii.), the "*three months*" there (xxviii. 11), and the "*two whole years*" in Rome (xxviii. 30).

These notes of time show that somebody must have kept a diary, and that journeys and sojourns were carefully recorded. Back of that was the belief of these men that their lives were God-planned. When we all believe that, the calendar will be consecrated.

PURPOSE

Various views have been held regarding the purpose of the Acts, some seeing in it a political tendency, some a doctrinal tendency, some an irenical tendency, and some a biographical tendency. Undoubtedly the last of these is the right view. In the other views the theories are brought into the Book, but in the last view the Book supplies the theory (i. 1-8). In this introduction the writer plainly indicates both the purpose and the plan of the record. As to *purpose*, it is to show that He Who did and taught on earth is now doing and teaching from heaven (1) ; and as to the *plan*, it is to show how Christianity developed and spread from Jerusalem, through Judea and Samaria, to "the uttermost part of the earth" (8). It is true that the record shows that opposition to early Christianity came rather from the Jews than from the Romans ; and it is also true that there are some striking parallels between the work of Peter and of Paul, such as the healing of a lame man (iii. 2, and xiv. 8), the raising of the dead (ix. 37, 40, and xx. 9,10), and the pronouncement of a judgment (v. 1, and xiii. 6). These particulars, however, do not indicate a "tendency," but naturally fall within the scope of the writer's main purpose, which is to show how the Christian missionary movement spread from Jerusalem to Rome, in a single generation, mainly through the instrumentality of two men, Peter and Paul. This progress of Christianity is clearly traced throughout, as the following passages show :—

" The Lord added to the Church day by day them that were being saved " (ii. 47).

10

" Believers were the more added to the Lord, multitudes of men and women " (v. 14-16).

" The Word of the Lord increased and the number of the disciples multiplied in Jersualem exceedingly, and a great number of the priests were obedient to the faith " (vi. 7).

" So the Church throughout all Judaea and Samaria and Galilee had peace, being edified, and walking in the fear of the Lord, and in the comfort of the Holy Spirit, was multiplied " (ix. 31).

" The Word of the Lord grew and multiplied " (xiii. 24).

" So the Churches were strengthened in the faith, and increased in number daily " (xvi. 5).

" So mightily grew the Word of God and prevailed " (xix. 20).

These seven summaries amply indicate the author's purpose, a purpose which is carried out in the whole plan of the Book.

ANALYSIS.

I. THE JEWISH PERIOD OF THE CHURCH'S WITNESS

Chapters i. 1-viii. 4. A.D. 30-35.

Central City, JERUSALEM.

1. FOUNDING OF THE CHURCH, i. 1-ii. 13.
   (i.) The Days of Preparation, i. 1-26.
   (ii.) The Day of Pentecost, ii. 1-13.

2. TESTIMONY OF THE CHURCH, ii. 14-47.
   (i.) Their Simple Creed, 14-41.
       The Discourse of Peter.
   (ii.) Their Sanctified Conduct, 42-47.
       A Description of the First Church.

3. OPPOSITION TO THE CHURCH, iii. 1-iv. 31.
   (i.) The Occasion of it, iii. 1-26.
   (ii.) The Expression of it, iv. 1-22.
   (iii.) The Sequel to it, iv. 23-31.

4. DISCIPLINE IN THE CHURCH, iv. 32-v. 16.
   (i.) The Originating Circumstances, iv. 32-37.
   (ii.) The Specific Occasion, v. 1-10.
   (iii.) The Salutary Effect, v. 11-16.

5. TESTING OF THE CHURCH, v. 17-42.
   (i.) The Detention and Deliverance of the Apostles, 17-21a.
   (ii.) The Trial and Triumph of the Apostles, 21b-42.

6. ADMINISTRATION IN THE CHURCH, vi. 1-6.
   (i.) The Complaint of the Disciples, 1.
   (ii.) The Conference of the Church, 2-4.
   (iii.) The Choice of Deacons, 5-6.

7. PERSECUTION OF THE CHURCH, vi. 7-viii. 4.
   (i.) The Reason for it, vi. 7.
   (ii.) The Focus of it, vi. 8-viii. 1a.
   (iii.) The Result of it, viii. 1b-4.

II. THE TRANSITION PERIOD OF THE CHURCH'S WITNESS

Chapters viii. 5–xii. 25. A.D. 35-44.

Central City, ANTIOCH.

1. PHILIP'S PREPARATION FOR THE WIDER WITNESS, viii. 5-40.
   - (i.) The Gospel at Samaria, 5-25.
     - (a) Under Philip, 5-13.
     - (b) Under the Apostles, 14-25.
   - (ii.) The Gospel toward Africa, 26-40.

2. SAUL'S PREPARATION FOR THE WIDER WITNESS, ix. 1-31.
   - (i.) The Conversion of Saul, 1-9.
   - (ii.) The Consecration of Saul, 10-19a.
   - (iii.) The Confession of Saul, 19b-21.
   - (iv.) The Conspiracy against Saul, 22-31.

3. PETER'S PREPARATION FOR THE WIDER WITNESS, ix. 32–x. 48.
   - (i.) Peter at Lydda, ix. 32-35.
   - (ii.) Peter at Joppa, ix. 36–x. 23a.
   - (iii.) Peter at Caesarea, x. 23b-48.

4. THE APOSTLES' PREPARATION FOR THE WIDER WITNESS, xi. 1-18.
   - (i.) The Complaint against Peter, 1-3.
   - (ii.) The Circumstances of Gentile blessing rehearsed, 4-17.
   - (iii.) The Conclusion of the Apostles, 18.

5. THE CHURCH'S PREPARATION FOR THE WIDER WITNESS, xi. 19–xii. 25
   - (i.) Progress of the Church at Antioch, xi. 19-30.
   - (ii.) Persecution of the Church at Jerusalem, xii. 1-23.
   - (iii.) Prosperity of the Church in general, xii. 24,25.

III. THE GENTILE PERIOD OF THE CHURCH'S WITNESS

Chapters xiii.-xxviii. A.D. 44-63.

Central City, ROME.

1. PAUL'S TIRELESS ACTIVITIES.

Chapters xiii. 1–xxi. 16. A.D. 44-58.

    (i) THE FIRST MISSIONARY JOURNEY.

        Chapters xiii.1–xv. 35, A.D.45-51.

        (a) The Call and Consecration at Antioch. xiii. 1-3.

        (b) The Circuit in Asia Minor, xiii. 4–xiv. 28.

        (1) The Outward Journey, xiii. 4–xiv. 20.
            A.S.S.P.P.A.I.L.D.

        (2) The Inward Journey, xiv. 21–28.
            L.I.A.P.A.A.

        (c) The Conference at Jerusalem, xv. 1-35.

    (ii.) THE SECOND MISSIONARY JOURNEY.

        Chapters xv. 36–xviii. 22. A.D. 51-54.

        (a) Apostolic Labours in Asia Minor, xv. 36-xvi. 10.
            A.S.C.D.L.P.G.T.

        (b) Apostolic Labours in Macedonia, xvi. 11–xvii. 15.
            S.N.P.A.A.T.B.

        (c) Apostolic Labours in Achaia, xvii. 15–xviii. 22.
            A.C.C.E.C.J.A.

        1 Thessalonians. A.D. 52. From Corinth.

        2 Thessalonians. A.D. 53. From Corinth.

    (iii.) THE THIRD MISSIONARY JOURNEY.

        Chapters xviii. 23–xxi. 16. A.D. 54-58.

        (a) Paul's Activities in Asia. xviii. 23–xix. 41.
            A.G.P.E.

1 Corinthians. A.D. 57. From Ephesus.

(b) Paul's Experiences in Europe. xx. 1-6.
M.A.P.

2 Corinthians. A.D. 57. From Macedonia.

Galatians. A.D. 58. From Corinth.

Romans. A.D. 58. From Corinth.

(c) Paul's Journey to Jerusalem, xx. 6–xxi. 16.
T.A.M.C.S.M.C.R.P.T.P.C.J.

2. PAUL'S FRUITFUL CAPTIVITIES.

Chapters xxi. 17–xxviii. 31. A.D. 58-63.

(i.) AT JERUSALEM, xxi. 17–xxiii. 35. A.D. 58.

(a) The Apostle's Detention, xxi. 17-36.

(b) The Apostle's Defence, xxi. 37–xxiii. 11.

(c) The Apostle's Danger, xxiii. 12-35.

(ii.) AT CAESAREA, xxiv.-xxvi. A.D. 58-60.

(a) Paul before Felix, xxiv.

(b) Paul before Festus, xxv. 1-12.

(c) Paul before Agrippa, xxv. 13–xxv. 32.

(iii.) AT ROME, xxvii.-xxviii. A.D. 61-63.

(a) On the Sea, xxvii.

(b) At the Island, xxviii. 1-10.

(c) In the City, xxviii. 11-31.

Ephesians A.D. 62. **Colossians** A.D. 62.

Philemon A.D. 62. **Philippians** A.D. 63.

Released from First Roman Imprisonment, A.D. 63-67.

1 Timothy A.D. 66–67. From Macedonia.

Titus A.D. 66–67. From Ephesus.

Re-arrested, Taken to Rome.

2 Timothy. A.D. 68.

Martyred at Rome, A.D. 68.

VALUES.

A work such as this has many and great values. There is the *Historical Value of the Acts*. It was fashionable at one time to call its historical accuracy into question, and even to deny it, but that day has passed, and never more so than now was this book regarded by scholars as of the highest historical value, thanks largely to Lightfoot and Ramsay. The latter writer says that he began the study of the trustworthiness of the Acts " with a mind unfavourable to it," and he ended that study by " placing this great writer on the high pedestal that belongs to him." Harnack also has been won over. In his *The Acts of the Apostles*, he says, " The book has now been restored to the position of credit which is its rightful due." Headlam says, " The investigators of the last twenty or thirty years have tended more and more to confirm the accuracy of the writer. In almost every point where we can follow him, even in minute details, he is right " ; and A. T. Robertson says that Luke's veracity has been triumphantly vindicated where once it was challenged, and that, " his character as a historian is firmly established in the passages where outside contact has been found." For illustrations of this see *The International Standard Bible Encyclopaedia*, vol. i, pp. 44, 45, *Hasting's Bible Dictionary*, vol. i, pp. 31, 32, and Paley's *Horae Paulinae*, an old but still most valuable work. The reader who has not time for nor access to these and other works on this subject can rest perfectly assured that this Book is everywhere true.

Then there is the *Dispensational Value of the Acts*. Suppose we had not this record, would it be possible for us to understand the Epistles on the background of the Old Testament ? In the former we have Christianity, and in the latter we have Judaism, but without the Acts we could not know how the one came to supersede the other, how the Church displaced the Temple and synagogue, and how national privileges yielded to world-wide blessing.

The Acts is probably the most important dispensational book in the Bible, for it tells us how the great change-over was made. In its pages we see that one dispensation is going and that another is coming, that Judaism is less and less, and Christianity more and more; it is a story both terminal and germinal, it is the hinge on which two ages swing, one out and the other in. One has only to study side by side Peter's sermon at Jerusalem on the day of Pentecost, and Paul's at Antioch in Pisidia (ii., xiii.), to see the change of viewpoint. Mark carefully what happened between these two sermons, the manifold preparation for the wider witness (see Analysis).

The Jewish element dominates in the first part of the Book (i.-vii.), the Gentile element in the last part (xiii.-xxviii.), and the way from the one to the other is explained in the middle part (viii.-xii.)

Again, there is the *Doctrinal Value of the Acts.* We may not look in this brief record of Christianity within the limits of a single generation, and that, following immediately on the Ascension of Jesus, for any development of doctrine ; that came later ; but, on the other hand, we are not to suppose that the Church at the beginning was without doctrine. The time for the formulation of creeds had not arrived, but in the apostolic preaching is found the very essence of any Christian Creed. It is not necessary for one to know much in order to become spiritually strong and powerful, but what is known must be of vital significance. What was it then, the Apostles believed and preached which made them such a power, and wrought such a change within so short a time ? In the main, four things—that Jesus was the Messiah, that His death was redemptive, that He rose from the dead, and that, by His Spirit, He was present with His people. That is a very simple but a very powerful creed. There are some seventeen discourses in the Acts, longer or shorter, and these facts and truths are the substance of them all. Not all at once did even the Apostles grasp the far-reaching implications of these truths, but what they did see they held firmly and preached boldly.

17

Further, there is the *Spiritual Value of the Acts*. The book discloses the true character of the Christian Church and the secret of her life and service. More and more it came to be seen that the Church was not something grafted on to the Temple or the synagogue, but was a Spiritual Institution, a Holy Society, indwelt, empowered, and guided by the Holy Spirit. The book is, really, the Acts of the Holy Spirit, He dominates the record. He is the Spirit of Promise (i), of Power (ii), of Healing (iii), of Boldness (iv), of Judgment (v), of Administration (vi), of Steadfastness (vii), of Evangelism (viii), of Comfort (ix), of Guidance (x), of Prophecy (xi), of Deliverance (xii), of Missions (xiii), of Protection (xiv), of Councils (xv), of Restraint and Constraint (xvi), of Opportunity (xvii), of Revelation (xviii), of Purpose (xix), of Ordination (xx), and so forth to the end.

It was about the Spirit that Jesus spoke to His apostles just before He ascended (i. 2, 4, 5, 8), it was the Spirit that came upon them at Pentecost (ii. 4), it is the Spirit that is promised to all who believe (ii. 38, 39), it was to the Spirit that Annaias and Sapphira lied (v. 3, 4, 9), it was with the Spirit that the apostles witnessed (v. 32), the first deacons had to be filled with the Spirit (vi 3, 5), Philip was instructed in the Spirit to speak to the eunuch (viii. 29), the Spirit bade Peter go to Cornelius (x. 19, xi. 12), the Spirit instructed the Church to send forth Barnabas and Saul on missionary work (xiii. 2, 4), it was the Spirit with the Apostles who settled the Jewish-Gentile controversy (xv. 28), and so all through the story. The Acts is the record of a Spirit-begotten, Spirit-filled, Spirit-guided Church, and that accounts for what she accomplished in those days. It is when the Church finds substitutes for the Holy Spirit that she is ineffective and defeated.

Again, there is the *Biographical Value of the Acts*. Like the *Pilgrim's Progress*, this Book is crowded with characters of all kinds, and the originals of some of Bunyan's characters are here. The outstanding personalities are, of course, Peter and Paul, and these are in the fellowship of a host of Christians, most of whom are unnamed. And there are foes here as well as friends, and women as well as men. What a Gallery ! Æneas, Agabus, Agrippa, Alexander, Ananias, Annas, Andrew, Apollos, Aquilla, Aristarchus, Augustus, Bar-Jesus Barnabas, Barsabas, Bartholomew, Bernice, Blastus, Caiaphas, Candace, Caesar, Claudius, Cornelius, Crispus, Damaris, Demettrius, Dionysius, Dorcas, Drusilla, Erastus, Eutychus, Felix, Festus, Gaius, Gallio, Gamaliel, Herod, James, Jason, Jesus, John Mark, John, Lucius, Lydia, Manaen, Mary, Matthew, Matthias, Mnason, Nicanor, Nicolas, Niger, Parmenas, Paulus, Priscilla, Prochorus, Publius, Rhoda, Sapphira, Sceva, Sergius Paulus, Secundus, Silas, Simeon, Simon, Sopater, Sosthenes, Stephen, Tabitha, Theophilus, Theudas, Timon, Timotheus, Trophimus, Tychicus, Tyrannus, and possibly others. This is a crowded platform and a stirring scene. To know these people is to know the history of the Christian Church from A.D. 30-63.

Just a word must be said on the *Missionary Value of the Acts.* Having all the circumstances in view, it is not too much to say that this is the greatest missionary story that has ever been told, and it must ever remain the authorized Missionary Manual of the Church. There has been a great development of missionary activity since that day, but still all that is vital for effective service throughout the world is found in the pages of the Acts.

It shows, to begin with, that the Christian Church is missionary, that Christianity is necessarily a self-propagating religion, it cannot be localized anywhere in a sense in which it cannot be localized everywhere ; if it did not spread it would die. Palgrave has said that Mohammedanism flourishes wherever the palm grows, and that is about the scope of it, but Christianity flourishes wherever human beings are. We have only to run over the names of the places mentioned in the Acts to be convinced of the missionary character of Christianity. Here are some of them : Jerusalem, Ephesus,

Corinth, Athens, Rome, and Antioch, Amphipolis, Antipatris, Apollonia, Assos, Attalia, Azotus, Berea, Caesarea, Cenchrea, Chios, Clauda, Cnidus, Cos, Crete, Cyprus, Damascus, Derbe, Gaza, Iconium, Joppa, Lystra, Lydda, Mileta, Miletus, Mitylene, Myra, Mysia, Neapolis, Paphos, Patara, Perga, Philippi, Ptolemais, Puteoli, Regium, Rhodes, Salamis, Samaria, Samos, Samothrace, Seleucia, Sidon, Syracuse, Tarsus, Thessalonica, Tyre, Troas, and other places, every one of which tells a bit of the first story of Christianity. The loss of the Acts would be irreparable.

Surely we feel the thrill of these names, which represent so much of the intellectual, political, and commercial life of the ancient world. Look at a map of Paul's travels long enough and steadily enough to be deeply impressed by the fact that because God loved all the world He commanded His disciples to " go into all the world, and preach the Gospel to every creature."

But when we come from the broad fact to the details we still find that the Acts is a Text Book of first rate importance. For instance, we see from it that this great enterprise had a home base. It was at Antioch in Syria that Barnabas and Saul were called to the work of world evangelism, and it was to Antioch that they returned and " rehearsed all things that God had done with them " (xiii. 1–3, xiv. 26–28). Furthermore, it was the whole Church in Antioch that sent them out, because, in fact, the whole Church was a Missionary Society.

Then, we see that in his journeyings Paul chose strategic places for the delivery of his message— Antioch, Iconium, Lystra, Derbe, Ephesus, Athens, and other places of like importance—in the belief that if Christianity were established in the centre it would spread to the circumference, that if the cities were captured the villages would be evangelized from these.

Again, wherever the missionaries went churches were established which became self-governing and self-supporting. Christian Jews were not sent out from Jerusalem or Antioch to take charge of these churches, but elders were ordained, instruction given, and they were left to build up and extend the good work (xiv. 21–23). Also, these churches were taught the great principle of Christian giving, and especially to care for their poorer brethren (cf. 2 Cor. viii.–ix.).

The message and the manner, as well as the method of these missionaries, are full of instruction for the present-day enterprise. Wherever they went they preached the Gospel, and did so tactfully. Their first care was for the souls of the heathen, and not for their physical or temporal welfare. We may be sure that if Paul lived to-day he would rejoice in Medical, Educational and Industrial Missions, but we may be equally sure that he would be vigorously opposed to any of these taking precedence of Evangelistic Missions. Those days had their temporal problems as well as these, but the missionaries always put first things first. A valuable study of this whole subject will be found in *Missionary Methods, St. Paul's and Ours*, by Roland Allen.

SUMMARIES

The following tables will help the student of the Apostolic Age to see how the Writings are related to one another in time and substance. The dates given must not be regarded as fixed and final, but they are near enough for working purposes.

I.
CHRONOLOGY OF NEW TESTAMENT LITERATURE

Decade	Writing	Date	Place	Period
A.D. 40–50	*James*	44–45	Jerusalem	
50–60	*1 Thessalonians*	52	Corinth	INITIAL
	2 Thessalonians	53	Corinth	
	1 Corinthians	57	Ephesus	
	2 Corinthians	57	Macedonia	
	Galatians	58	Corinth	
	Romans	58	Corinth	
50–65	*Mark*	50–65	Rome	
	Matthew	50–65	Judea	
	Luke	50–65	Caesarea	
60–70	*Ephesians*	62–63	Rome	CENTRAL
	Colossians	62–63	Rome	
	Philemon	62–63	Rome	
	Philippians	63	Rome	
	1 Peter	62–64	Babylon ?	
	2 Peter	64	Rome ?	
	Acts	64–66	Rome	
	Hebrews	64–66	Rome	
	Jude	65–68	Jerusalem	
	1 Timothy	65–67	Macedonia	
	Titus	65–67	Ephesus ?	
	2 Timothy	67–68	Rome	
90–100	*John's Gospel*	90– 95	Ephesus	FINAL
	John's Epistles	90–95	Ephesus	
	Revelation	96	Patmos	

II.
THE PAULINE LETTERS
(i) As to ORDER.   A.D. 50–70.

Letter	Date	Letter	Date
1 Thessalonians	52	*Ephesians*	62
2 Thessalonians	53	*Colossians*	62
1 Corinthians	57	*Philemon*	62
2 Corinthians	57	*Philippians*	63
Galatians	57–8	*1 Timothy*	67
Romans	58	*Titus*	67
(Hebrews)		*2 Timothy*	68

(ii) As to DESTINATION

To CHURCHES	To INDIVIDUALS
Thessalonica (2) *Corinth* (2) *Galatian Group* *Rome* *Ephesus* *Colossae* *Philippi*	*Philemon* *Timothy* (2) *Titus*

(iii) As to SETTING

LETTER	PERIOD	"ACTS"
1 *Thessalonians* 2 *Thessalonians*	*Second Missionary Journey* ,, ,, ,,	xviii. 11 xviii. 11

1 *Corinthians*
 2 *Corinthians*
 Galatians
 Romans
	Third Missionary Journey
	   ,, ,, ,,
	   ,, ,, ,,
	   ,, ,, ,,
		xix. 20, 21
		 xx. 1
		 xx. 2, 3
		 xx. 2, 3

Ephesians
 Colossians
 Philemon
 Philippians
	First Roman Captivity
	   ,, ,, ,,
	   ,, ,, ,,
	   ,, ,, ,,
		xxviii. 30
		 xxviii. 30
		 xxviii. 30
		 xxviii. 30

1 *Timothy* *Titus* 2 *Timothy*	*Fourth Missionary Journey* ,, ,, ,, *Second Roman Captivity*	1 Tim. i. 3 Titus 1. 5 2 Tim. iv. 20

(iv) As to CHARACTER

GROUP	LETTER	CHARACTERISTIC
A *PREFACE* A.D. 52–53	1–2 *Thessalonians*	*Prophetical* *Christian Hope* *The Coming* *Perfecting of Salvation*
B *THE CROSS* A.D. 57–58	1–2 *Corinthians* *Galatians* *Romans*	*Polemical* *Christian Faith* *The Conflict* *Plan of Salvation*
C *THE CHRIST* A.D. 62–63	*Ephesians* *Colossians* *Philemon* *Philippians*	*Philosophical* *Christian Love* *The Conquest* *Privileges of Salvation*
D *POSTSCRIPT* A.D. 67–68	1 *Timothy* *Titus* 2 *Timothy*	*Pastoral* *Hope, Faith, Love* *The Congregation* *Purpose of Salvation*

Observe how these letters go in pairs.

1.	{ 1 *Thessalonians* { 2 *Thessalonians*	.HOPE
2.	{ 1 *Corinthians* { 2 *Corinthians*	CONDUCT
3.	{ *Galatians* { *Romans*	TRUTH
4.	{ *Ephesians* { *Colossians*	LIFE
5.	{ *Philemon* { *Philippians*	UNITY
6.	{ *Timothy* { *Titus*	SERVICE

LITERATURE

The literature on this Book is vast, and all that we do here is to recommend a few of the best books for the general reader.

Farrar, *Early Days of Christianity* ; *Life and Work of St. Paul* ; Paley, *Horae Paulinae* ; Ramsay, *St. Paul the Traveller and the Roman Citizen* ; *Cities of St. Paul* ; *Luke the Physician, and Other Studies* ; *The Church in the Roman Empire* ; Smith, *Voyage and Shipwreck of St. Paul* ; A. T. Robertson, *Epochs in the Life of Paul* ; *Word Pictures in the New Testament*; vol. viii. Conybeare and Howson, *St. Paul.*

In addition to these there are the Commentaries for those who have access to them, especially *The Pulpit Commentary*, Ellicott's, and Matthew Henry's ; and also the articles in the Bible Dictionaries which bear on the whole subject of the Church in the first century, articles on *The Acts, Paul, Peter, Luke, The Christian Church*, etc.

But nothing can be a substitute for the repeated prayerful reading of the Acts itself.

Title : A NEW STORY BEGINS

1 The former treatise have I made, O Theophilus, of all that Jesus began both to do and teach, 2 Until the day in which he was taken up, after that he through the Holy Ghost had given commandments unto the apostles whom he had chosen : 3 To whom also he shewed himself alive after his passion by many infallible proofs, being seen of them forty days and speaking of the things pertaining to the kingdom of God : 4 And, being assembled together with them, commanded them that they should not depart from Jerusalem, but wait for the promise of the Father, which, saith he, ye have heard of me. 5 For John truly baptized with water ; but ye shall be baptized with the Holy Ghost not many days hence.

6 When they therefore were come together, they asked of him, saying, Lord, wilt thou at this time restore again the kingdom to Israel ? 7 And he said unto them, It is not for you to know the times or the seasons, which the Father put in his own power. 8 But ye shall receive power, after that the Holy Ghost is come upon you : and ye shall be witnesses unto me both in Jerusalem, and in all Judæa, and in Samaria, and unto the uttermost part of the earth. 9 And when he had spoken these things, while they beheld, he was taken up ; and a cloud received him out of their sight. 10 And while they looked stedfastly toward heaven as he went up, behold, two men stood by them in white apparel ; 11 Which also said, Ye men of Galilee, why stand ye gazing up into heaven ? this same Jesus, which is taken up from you into heaven, shall so come in like manner as ye have seen him go into heaven.

EXPOSITION

The author of this Book is Luke, a Gentile, and the only Gentile writer of Holy Scripture. He was a medical doctor, and a man of considerable culture. Observe also that he dedicates both the " Gospel " and the " Acts " to Theophilus, another Gentile, and probably a Roman official. The name (" loved of God ") is not a generic term for all Christians, but that of a friend of Luke's. These two names indicate the point of view of Luke's two Writings, namely, that the Gospel of Jesus Christ is for the world, and that the Church of God is catholic, composed of believers " *of all nations, and kindreds, and people, and tongues.*"

In entering upon the study of this Book these particulars should be registered. (a) *The Author*, Luke, the writer of the " Gospel " (1). (b) *Date*, A.D. 63. (c) *Subject*. The origin and progress of Christianity from the capital of Judaism to the capital of Heathenism. The Acts of the glorified Saviour in the planting and training of His Church, or, as a negro Christian said, " This is a book of Words about Deeds." (d) *Place of writing*, Rome. (e) *Period covered*, A.D. 30–63.

The general outline is,

1. Founding of the Church : *the Jewish period of her witness* (i. 1 to viii. 4). 2. Broadening of the Church : *the Transitional period of her witness* (viii. 5 to xii. 25). 3. Extending of the Church : *the Gentile period of her witness* (xiii. 1 to xxviii. 31). Peter dominates part one ; Paul dominates part three ; and both of them are prominent in part two. Jerusalem is the city focus in part one ; Antioch, in part two ; and Rome, in part three. Part one extends from A.D. 30–35 ; Part two, A.D. 35–44 ; Part three, A.D. 44–63. Enter these particulars in your Bible.

The subject of chapter one, is, (a) Preparation for the Church, covering a period of *ten* days (5), which with the forty days with Jesus, after the resurrection (3), made the fifty days between the Passover and Pentecostal Feasts (Lev. xxiii. 15). This preparation was made in two ways : first, by *Christ's ascension* (1–11) ; then, by *prayerful waiting* on the part of the disciples (12–26). There is no need for us now-a-days to wait for the Holy Spirit ; the fact is that He is waiting for us. Consider then, first of all, *Christ's Ascension* (1–11).

Here we see that the " Acts " is a sequel to, and continuation of, the Gospel Records. Verse 3 connects with the *Resurrection* at the end of " Matthew " ; verse 9, 10, with the *Ascension* at the end of " Mark " ; verses 7, 8, with the *Promise of the Spirit* at the end of " Luke "; and verse 11 anticipates the *Second Advent* at the end of " John." Mark these great notes : CHRIST'S LIFE (1), DEATH (3), RESURRECTION (3), KINGDOM (3, 6, 7), SPIRIT (4, 5, 8), ASCENSION (9–11), and SECOND ADVENT (11), covering a period of 2,000 years.

When Jesus said, " It is finished," He did not mean that His work was finished. There is a sense in which it is entirely wrong to speak of " the finished work of Christ." Luke says that the " Gospel " he wrote told only of what " *Jesus began to do and teach*," the natural inference from which is that in the " Acts " he is going to record something of what Jesus, now the risen Lord, is continuing to do and teach, and as this record is only the first chapter of Church history, it is clear that Christ is still doing and teaching. The difference between the *beginning* and the *continuing* is that *then* He wrought in person here on earth, and *now* He is working from heaven by His Spirit, in and through His Church. Christ's departure was not a sunset, but a sunrise.

Verse 8 is the key to the Book, telling, as it does, of the Central Subject of Christian Witness, *Christ* : the Widening Sphere, from Jerusalem to the " *uttermost part of the earth* " : the Exclusive Source, " *ye*," the Christian Church ; and the Unfailing Secret, " *the Holy Spirit*." Wonderful ! Wonderful !

Thought : IT IS POWER THAT FIRST IS PROMISED (8).

THE ACTS i. 12–26

Title : WAITING DAYS

12 Then returned they unto Jerusalem from the mount called Olivet, which is from Jerusalem a sabbath day's journey. 13 And when they were come in, they went up into an upper room, where abode both Peter, and James, and John, and Andrew, Philip, and Thomas, Bartholomew, and Matthew, James the son of Alphæus, and Simon Zelotes, and Judas the brother of James. 14 These all continued with one accord in prayer and supplication, with the women, and Mary the mother of Jesus, and with his brethren.

15 And in those days Peter stood up in the midst of the disciples, and said, (the number of names together were about an hundred and twenty,) 16 Men and brethren, this scripture must needs have been fulfilled, which the Holy Ghost by the mouth of David spake before concerning Judas, which was guide to them that took Jesus. 17 For he was numbered with us, and had obtained part of this ministry. 18 Now this man purchased a field with the reward of iniquity ; and falling headlong, he burst asunder in the midst, and all his bowels gushed out. 19 And it was known unto all the dwellers at Jerusalem ; insomuch as that field is called in their proper tongue, Aceldama, that is to say, The field of blood. 20 For it is written in the book of Psalms, Let his habitation be desolate, and let no man dwell therein : and his bishoprick let another take.

21 Wherefore of these men which have companied with us all the time that the Lord Jesus went in and out among us, 22 Beginning from the baptism of John, unto that same day that he was taken up from us, must one be ordained to be a witness with us of his resurrection. 23 And they appointed two, Joseph called Barsabas, who was surnamed Justus, and Matthias. 24 And they prayed, and said, Thou, Lord, which knowest the hearts of all men, shew whether of these two thou hast chosen, 25 That he may take part of this ministry and apostleship, from which Judas by transgression fell, that he might go to his own place. 26 And they gave forth their lots ; and the lot fell upon Matthias ; and he was numbered with the eleven apostles.

EXPOSITION

Our attention is here called to 1. A MOMENTOUS PRAYER MEETING. The founding of the Church was prepared for, not only by Christ's ascension (9–11), but by prayerful waiting on the part of the disciples (12–14). The "*upper room*" (13), and "*one place*" (ii. 1), was, without doubt, where they had kept the Passover nearly six weeks before (Luke xxii. 12). The prayer-meeting lasted for ten days (i. 5 ; ii. 1), and was attended by all the Apostles, except Judas Iscariot, who was dead ; by certain women, including the mother of Jesus, of whom we never read again ; and also by Jesus' brothers, who now at last believed (John vii. 5). What were they waiting for these ten days ? See verses 4, 5. The Father's promise was fulfilled 1900 years ago, so that our duty now is, not to *wait*, but to take.

Now follows a most important event. The Divinely appointed number of the Apostles was *Twelve*, and the number of the Tribes of Israel was *Twelve*, which, together are represented by the *Four and Twenty Elders* of Revelation iv. 4. As Judas was dead (16—20), it was necessary that some one be appointed to take his place (21, 22), which, at this time, was done (23–26).

Consider then, 2. THE DEATH AND DOOM OF JUDAS (16-20, 25,). Peter's explanation in verses 16, 17, is for the information of the "hundred and twenty" (15), and not for his brother apostles. Verses 18, 19 are a parenthesis added by the historian Luke. Read this with Matt. xxvii. 3–8. The accounts are not contradictory, if we assume that *the rope broke* with which he hanged himself. Make a note of Peter's interpretation of Psalm lxix. 25.

3. Now follows THE APPOINTMENT OF A NEW APOSTLE (21–26). Mark the necessary qualification (21, 22) : "*All the time . . . beginning from . . . unto.*" Observe "*put forward*," not "*appointed*," in verse 23. It says, "*Thou hast*," not, "*Thou wilt*," in verse 24. "*Part*" in verse 25 should be "*place*," then we see the place Judas forfeited, and the place he acquired. Very solemn. Beware ! Matthias was elected. Did the Apostles do right in adopting the procedure which resulted in the appoint-

29

ment of Matthias ? At any rate we hear no more of him in Scripture, and references to him in tradition are not to his credit. Paul in reality filled the place. Did God appoint you to the office which you hold ? Then, don't talk about resigning.

Thought : *OUR PLACE IN ETERNITY IS DETERMINED IN TIME* (25).

THE ACTS ii. 1–13

Title : THE DAY OF PENTECOST

1 And when the day of Pentecost was fully come, they were all with one accord in one place. 2 And suddenly there came a sound from heaven as of a rushing mighty wind, and it filled all the house where they were sitting. 3 And there appeared unto them cloven tongues like as of fire, and it sat upon each of them. 4 And they were all filled with the Holy Ghost, and began to speak with other tongues, as the Spirit gave them utterance.

5 And there were dwelling at Jerusalem Jews, devout men, out of every nation under heaven. 6 Now when this was noised abroad, the multitude came together, and were confounded, because that every man heard them speak in his own language. 7 And they were all amazed and marvelled, saying one to another, Behold, are not all these which speak Galilæans ? 8 And how hear we every man in our own tongue, wherein we were born ? 9 Parthians, and Medes, and Elamites, and the dwellers in Mesopotamia, and in Judæa, and Cappadocia, in Pontus, and Asia, 10 Phrygia, and Pamphylia, in Egypt, and in the parts of Libya about Cyrene, and strangers of Rome, Jews and proselytes, 11 Cretes and Arabians, we do hear them speak in our tongues the wonderful works of God. 12 And they were all amazed, and were in doubt, saying one to another, What meaneth this ? 13 Others mocking said, These men are full of new wine.

EXPOSITION

After the ten days comes the great Day, the Birthday of the Christian Church (1–13). There were *Christians* before Pentecost (i. 13, 15. 1 Cor. xv. 6), but on this day they were constituted the Christian Church by the Descent and Baptism of the Holy Spirit : Christian believers became Christ's Body. In our portion are two main particulars.

1. THE MANIFESTATION OF THE SPIRIT(1-4). Observe carefully the *day*, the *company*, the *place*, the *sound*, the *light*, the *power*, and the *endowment*, seven things. A new dispensation was inaugurated on this day. True, all the members of the Church were Jews, during the first five or six years (so far as we know), but this was Christianity, and not Judaism. We may say that the *wind* symbolizes the spiritual constitution of the Church ; the *fire*, the individual possession of the Spirit ; and the *tongues*, the universal commission of the saved. Distinguish between the *Baptism* and the *Infilling* of the Spirit. Both blessings were vouchsafed on the Day of Pentecost ; but, whereas the Baptism is once for all, the Filling is oft repeated (cf. iv. 31). Baptism and Filling are opposite figures. In the former, the vessel is in the element ; in the latter, the element is also in the vessel. We are made Christians by the Baptism ; but we are made Christ-like by the Filling.

2. THE MARVEL OF THE PEOPLE (5-13). Let us clear up two popular misunderstandings here. (a) The *speech* is not the same throughout this passage (1-8). " Tongues " in 3, 4, is *glossai*, whence our word *glossary* : but in 6, 8, it is *dialektoi*, whence our word *dialects*. From this it is clear that the " tongues " of 1 Cor. xiv., were not known languages. (b) These Christians were not preaching the gospel (11). They did not speak because the crowd was there ; the crowd came there because they were speaking (6). The utterance was one of adoration of God the doer of wonderful things. Such will always be variously interpreted (12, 13).

Thought : " BE FILLED WITH THE SPIRIT."

31

THE ACTS ii. 14–24

Title : *A POWERFUL SERMON*

14 But Peter, standing up with the eleven, lifted up his voice, and said unto them, Ye men of Judæa, and all ye that dwell at Jerusalem, be this known unto you, and hearken to my words : **15** For these are not drunken, as ye suppose, seeing it is but the third hour of the day. **16** But this is that which was spoken by the prophet Joel ;

17 And it shall come to pass in the last days, saith God, I will pour out of my Spirit upon all flesh : and your sons and your daughters shall prophesy, and your young men shall see visions, and your old men shall dream dreams : **18** And on my servants and on my handmaidens I will pour out in those days of my Spirit ; and they shall prophesy : **19** And I will shew wonders in heaven above, and signs in the earth beneath ; blood, and fire, and vapour of smoke : **20** The sun shall be turned into darkness, and the moon into blood, before that great and notable day of the Lord come : **21** And it shall come to pass, that whosoever shall call on the name of the Lord shall be saved.

22 Ye men of Israel, hear these words ; Jesus of Nazareth, a man approved of God among you by miracles and wonders and signs, which God did by him in the midst of you, as ye yourselves also know : **23** Him, being delivered by the determinate counsel and foreknowledge of God, ye have taken, and by wicked hands have crucified and slain : **24** Whom God hath raised up, having loosed the pains of death : because it was not possible that he should be holden of it.

EXPOSITION

THE TESTIMONY OF THE CHURCH (14–47) follows immediately on the Founding of it. Mark here—Their Simple Creed : the Discourse of Peter (14–41), and Their Sanctified Conduct : a Description of the First Church (42–47).

(1) THEIR SIMPLE CREED (14–41). Peter's Sermon is in three main parts—introduction, argument, and conclusion. (i) THE INTRODUCTION (14–21). Here

32

is first, a *Defence* (14, 15), and then, a *Declaration* (16–21) : in the first he quashes, and in the second he quotes. Drunk! No Jew on the Sabbath, and that a Feast day, would either eat or drink before nine in the morning (15). The suggestion was preposterous. But Peter's declaration and explanation, " *this is that*," and the remainder of his introduction is a quotation from Joel ii. 28–32. The original is spoken only of Judah, but the scope of the prophecy is here enlarged, yet, it is not on this occasion full-filled ; for this, it still awaits a day to come. In the body of the Sermon, Peter takes his stand boldly on the *resurrection of Jesus.* If that can be proved, all is proved. If He who seven weeks before expired on Calvary is now alive, then, the Church is established, and must be triumphant.

Observe that in Peter's great (ii) ARGUMENT (22–35), the dominating facts are (a) *declared* (22–24), *predicted* (25–31), *attested* (32), and *proved* (33–35). The *Declaration* is that Jesus Christ *lived*, and *died*, and *rose again* (22–24). *He* lived His life (22) ; *men* compassed His death (23) ; and *God* raised Him from the dead (24). How great a word is this, " *it was not possible that He should be holden of death* " (24). Why, *not possible* ? Because He was God as well as man. Because He trusted His Father to raise Him up. Because the Scriptures cannot be broken. Because it is unthinkable that death and the devil should triumph. " *Thou wilt not leave my soul in Sheol, neither wilt Thou suffer Thy Holy One to see corruption.*" " IT WAS NOT POSSIBLE." The resurrection of Christ is the very heart of the Christian Gospel. Have you any doubt ?

Thought : THE TOMB IS EMPTY. HALLE-
        LUJAH !

THE ACTS ii. 25–36

Title : HOW TO PREACH

25 For David speaketh concerning him, I foresaw the Lord always before my face, for he is on my right

hand, that I should not be moved : 26 Therefore did my heart rejoice, and my tongue was glad ; moreover also my flesh shall rest in hope : 27 Because thou wilt not leave my soul in hell, neither wilt thou suffer thine Holy One to see corruption. 28 Thou hast made known to me the ways of life ; thou shalt make me full of joy with thy countenance.

29 Men and brethren, let me freely speak unto you of the patriarch David, that he is both dead and buried, and his sepulchre is with us unto this day. 30 Therefore being a prophet, and knowing that God had sworn with an oath to him that of the fruit of his loins, according to the flesh, he would raise up Christ to sit on his throne ; 31 He seeing this before spake of the resurrection of Christ, that his soul was not left in hell, neither his flesh did see corruption. 32 This Jesus hath God raised up, whereof we all are witnesses. 33 Therefore being by the right hand of God exalted, and having received of the Father the promise of the Holy Ghost, he hath shed forth this, which ye now see and hear. 34 For David is not ascended into the heavens : but he saith himself, The Lord said unto my Lord, Sit thou on my right hand, 35 Until I make thy foes thy footstool. 36 Therefore let all the house of Israel know assuredly, that God hath made that same Jesus, whom ye have crucified, both Lord and Christ.

EXPOSITION

(ii) THE ARGUMENT of Peter circles round the Resurrection of Jesus, which he has *declared to be a fact* (22-24), *predicted* (25-31), *attested* (32), and *proved* (33-35). Peter now shows that (b) *The Resurrection was predicted* (25-31). He just makes a quotation (25-28), and draws a conclusion (29-31). It is all very simple, and very powerful. Read Psalm xvi. 8-11. Observe that reference is made in the prediction to the Messiah's *soul*, which went to Sheol (Hades), and to His *body*, which was put in the tomb, but not to see corruption. The conclusion is conclusive. David's body did see corruption, so that it could not have been himself that he had referred to in the Psalm. Only One fulfilled these words, therefore David was a *prophet* (30), and a *seer* (31), and foretold an event which did not take place until 1,000 years later. As Abram looked for the City, David looked for the King.

Next, (c) *The Resurrection is Attested* (32) : " *we are all witnesses.*" " *All,*" at least one hundred and twenty (i. 15), and probably many more. Would any Court of Law refuse the testimony of one hundred and twenty eye-witnesses. No event in human history is better attested than the resurrection of Jesus Christ from the dead.

And finally, (d) *The Resurrection is Proved* (33–35). The proof is the Christian Church, consequent upon the gift of the Spirit, which " gift " was bestowed when Christ ascended, which He could not have done if He had not risen, which last fact is predicted in another Davidic Psalm (110).

Now mark (iii) The Conclusion of all this (36). " *Let every house of Israel therefore know assuredly* " —what ? " *that God hath made Him both Lord and Christ, this Jesus whom ye crucified.*" Observe carefully this designation. *Jesus* is His human name ; *Christ* is His official title ; and *Lord* is His Divine title. Jesus is both Christ and Lord, He is therefore the Lord Jesus Christ. That truly is a wonderful sermon ; and we shall see that it had a mighty effect.

Thought : *TRUTH SPOKEN WITH POWER IS SOMETHING TO RECKON WITH.*

THE ACTS ii. 37-47

Title : THE EARLY CHURCH

37 Now when they heard this, they were pricked in their heart, and said unto Peter and to the rest of the apostles, Men and brethren, what shall we do ? 38 Then Peter said unto them, Repent, and be baptized every one of you in the name of Jesus Christ for the remission of sins, and ye shall receive the gift of the Holy Ghost. 39 For the promise is unto you, and to your children, and to all that are

afar off, even as many as the Lord our God shall call. 40 And with many other words did he testify and exhort, saying, Save yourselves from this untoward generation. 41 Then they that gladly received his word were baptized : and the same day there were added unto them about three thousand souls. 42 And they continued stedfastly in the apostles' doctrine and fellowship, and in breaking of bread, and in prayers.

43 And fear came upon every soul : and many wonders and signs were done by the apostles. 44 And all that believed were together, and had all things common ; 45 And sold their possessions and goods, and parted them to all men, as every man had need. 46 And they, continuing daily with one accord in the temple, and breaking bread from house to house, did eat their meat with gladness and singleness of heart, 47 Praising God, and having favour with all the people. And the Lord added to the church daily such as should be saved.

EXPOSITION

We are not through with this Sermon yet, for so powerful was it that there had to be an after-meeting (37-41). " They were *pierced* in their heart " hearing of Him whom they had *pierced*, and conviction stimulated inquiry (37). Only they will ask " *what shall we do ?* " who are conscious to some extent of *what they have done.* Peter plainly points out to them the way of salvation : first of all, the TERMS of it (38), and then the SCOPE of it (39).

In the TERMS, two things are required of us, *repentance* and *confession* (38a), and one thing is promised by God, the *bestowment* of the Holy Spirit (38b). As to the SCOPE, the offer of salvation is *personal*, " as many as " ; *universal* " to all that are afar off " ; and *age-abiding*, " to you and to your children." Peter *testified* and *exhorted*, two things preachers should do every time they preach (40) ; and the proof that Christ has saved us will be that we shall " *save ourselves* " (40).

At the first proclamation of the Law, three thousand souls were slain (Exod. xxxii. 28) ; but at the first proclamation of the Gospel, three thousand were saved (41). They were not " *added* " in order to be saved, but because they were saved. Is that how you joined the Church?

After (1) The Church's Simple Creed (14–41), comes (2) Her Sanctified Conduct (42–47). Here is a precious picture of the early life of the Church. Observe what were the characteristics: *steadfastness* in the faith, *fellowship, prayer* (42), *fear* (43), *charity* (44, 45), *joy* (46), *praise, influence*, and *success* (47). Go over these again, and ask, ' How many of them characterize my Church? ' and ' What have I done, or am I doing to make the Church of to-day like the Church of that day? " Those whom " *the Lord added* " (47) were " *added to the Lord* " (v. 14). If you have been *added* by any other person, or in any other way, it is time you were *subtracted*.

Thought: ONLY A PURE CHURCH CAN BE POWERFUL AND PERMANENT.

THE ACTS iii. 1-10

Title: HELPLESSNESS AND HEALING

1 Now Peter and John went up together into the temple at the hour of prayer, being the ninth hour. 2 And a certain man lame from his mother's womb was carried, whom they laid daily at the gate of the temple which is called Beautiful, to ask alms of them that entered into the temple; 3 Who seeing Peter and John about to go into the temple asked an alms. 4 And Peter, fastening his eyes upon him with John, said, Look on us. 5 And he gave heed unto them, expecting to receive something of them. 6 Then Peter said, Silver and gold have I none; but such as I have give I thee: In the name of Jesus Christ of Nazareth rise up and walk. 7 And he took him by the right hand, and lifted him up: and immediately his feet and ancle bones received strength. 8 And he leaping up stood, and walked, and entered with them into the temple, walking, and leaping, and praising God. 9 And all the people

saw him walking and praising God : 10 And they knew that it was he which sat for alms at the Beautiful gate of the temple : and they were filled with wonder and amazement at that which had happened unto him.

EXPOSITION

In this story four things claim our attention.

1. THE CIRCUMSTANCES (1). It is interesting to find Peter and John together : opposites often well agree. Peter was practical ; John was mystical ; each had something which the other lacked, and so they could help one another ; and they did. Let us cultivate an interest in people who are different from ourselves, and so enrich ourselves. These two men were on the way to the Temple. The Christian Church did not at once break away from the Jewish Temple. There are no ruptures in the Kingdom of God. These men were going to public prayer at 3 p.m. Private prayer is not instead of, but in preparation for, public prayer. What we call the Prayer Meeting will be better attended and maintained when we all pray more and better in private.

2. THE CASE (2, 3). A man, forty years of age (iv. 22), lame from his birth, lying at the Gate Beautiful of the Temple, carried there, and daily, begging, asking for alms who needed legs. Mark those seven particulars. In his helplessness he illustrates the inability of us all, in our unregenerate state, to walk with God.

3. THE CURE (4–7). The Apostles looking on the man, bade him look on them. His expectation was aroused, but it did not rise higher than his physical need. Our need is always greater than we imagine it to be, and God's grace is also greater. He does for us " exceeding abundantly above all that we ask or think." " *Silver and gold have I none* " (6). The true wealth of the Church is not material, but spiritual. Peter was poor, and yet, how rich ! Can he ever be poor who has led a soul to Christ ! (ii. 41). " *Such as I have* " ; and that was vastly more than

he, at this time, imagined: see his Epistles. Well what should we do with what we have? What Peter did—"*give I thee.*" He who *has*, and *keeps*, will *lose*. Give what you have, and you will get. "*In the Name . . . rise up and walk.*" There was and is power in the Name. Plead it, and then lend a helping hand (6, 7).

4. THE CONSEQUENCES (8–10). The healed man was delirious with joy (8), and the people were dumb with wonder (9, 10). No doubt this miracle is introduced here because of its consequences for the Apostles and the Church (iv.). No event ends with itself.

Thought : IT IS BETTER TO LEAP UP THAN TO LIE ABOUT (viii. 2).

THE ACTS iii. 11-26

Title : A MESSAGE ON A MIRACLE

11 And as the lame man which was healed held Peter and John, all the people ran together unto them in the porch that is called Solomon's, greatly wondering. 12 And when Peter saw it, he answered unto the people, Ye men of Israel, why marvel ye at this? or why look ye so earnestly on us, as though by our own power or holiness we had made this man to walk? 13 The God of Abraham, and of Isaac, and of Jacob, the God of our fathers, hath glorified his Son Jesus; whom ye delivered up, and denied him in the presence of Pilate, when he was determined to let him go. 14 But ye denied the Holy One and the Just, and desired a murderer to be granted unto you; 15 And killed the Prince of life, whom God hath raised from the dead; whereof we are witnesses. 16 And his name through faith in his name hath made this man strong, whom ye see and know : yea, the faith which is by him hath given him this perfect soundness in the presence of you all.

17 And now, brethren, I wot that through ignorance ye did it, as did also your rulers. 18 But

those things, which God before had shewed by the mouth of all his prophets, that Christ should suffer, he hath so fulfilled. 19 Repent ye therefore, and be converted, that your sins may be blotted out, when the times of refreshing shall come from the presence of the Lord ; 20 And he shall send Jesus Christ, which before was preached unto you : 21 Whom the heaven must receive until the times of restitution of all things, which God hath spoken by the mouth of all his holy prophets since the world began. 22 For Moses truly said unto the fathers, A prophet shall the Lord your God raise up unto you of your brethren, like unto me ; him shall ye hear in all things whatsoever he shall say unto you. 23 And it shall come to pass, that every soul, which will not hear that prophet, shall be destroyed from among the people. 24 Yea, and all the prophets from Samuel and those that follow after, as many as have spoken, have likewise foretold of these days. 25 Ye are the children of the prophets, and of the covenant which God made with our fathers, saying unto Abraham, And in thy seed shall all the kindreds of the earth be blessed. 26 Unto you first God, having raised up his Son Jesus, sent him to bless you, in turning away every one of you from his iniquities.

EXPOSITION

Keep the sequence of this history in mind : FOUNDING OF THE CHURCH (i. 1 to ii. 13) ; WITNESS OF THE CHURCH (ii. 14–47) ; and now, OPPOSITION TO THE CHURCH (iii. 1 to iv. 31). Here mark *the occasion of* (iii. 1–26) ; *the expression of* (iv. 1–22) ; and *the sequel to this opposition* (iv. 23–41).

THE OCCASION OF THE OPPOSITION TO THE CHURCH was the healing of the cripple (iv. 16, 22). Here is Peter's *third address*, iii. 12–26, with which compare the first, i. 15–22 : and the second, ii. 14–26. The audience gave Peter a great opportunity (11, 12a): he saw the situation, and seized it. Always be on the look-out for opportunities, they are all around us. What did Peter " *answer* " ? (12). The people's state of mind. We can often answer when there is no verbal question ; eyes as well as mouths, can ask

40

questions. Peter answers by asking two questions, and in doing so, corrects two mistakes. The people *marvelled*; but why should they? Surely a great God can do great things. And they thought that the miracle was the work of the apostles, whereas Peter and John were but the agents (12).

Now follows some plain speaking: the people are charged with murder (13–15), but man's ruling God over-ruled: Whom they crucified He glorified; Whom they rejected He raised. When Peter charged these people with *denying* Jesus, he cannot but have remembered that he had done the same (13, 14).

There is power in Christ's Name, but it must be trusted to become operative (16). The solemn charge of verse 15 is somewhat softened by verse 17, yet the people were responsible and are called upon to repent (19). Though men act with perfect freedom, a Divine sovereignty runs through human history; the wicked as well as the worthy are employed for the working out of eternal designs (18, 24). And the end is not yet (19, 21).

Christ is the subject of all prophecy (24), and *salvation* is the greatest of all themes (26). Here is a striking word—" *God sent Him to bless you*,"—God, Him, you; and the blessing is in being *turned from* our sins, and *turned to* the Saviour (26). Are you turned?

Thought: ONLY THE CRUCIFIED CAN CONVERT (18, 19).

THE ACTS iv. 1-12

Title: THE APOSTLES BEFORE THE AUTHORITIES

1 And as they spake unto the people, the priests, and the captain of the temple, and the Sadducees, came upon them, 2 Being grieved that they taught

the people, and preached through Jesus the resurrection from the dead. 3 And they laid hands on them, and put them in hold unto the next day : for it was now eventide. 4 Howbeit many of them which heard the word believed ; and the number of the men was about five thousand.

5 And it came to pass on the morrow, that their rulers, and elders, and scribes, 6 And Annas the high priest, and Caiaphas, and John, and Alexander, and as many as were of the kindred of the high priest, were gathered together at Jerusalem. 7 And when they had set them in the midst, they asked, By what power, or by what name, have ye done this ? 8 Then Peter, filled with the Holy Ghost, said unto them, Ye rulers of the people, and elders of Israel, 9 If we this day be examined of the good deed done to the impotent man, by what means he is made whole ; 10 Be it known unto you all, and to all the people of Israel, that by the name of Jesus Christ of Nazareth, whom ye crucified, whom God raised from the dead, even by him doth this man stand here before you whole. 11 This is the stone which was set at nought of you builders, which is become the head of the corner. 12 Neither is there salvation in any other : for there is none other name under heaven given among men, whereby we must be saved.

EXPOSITION

If OPPOSITION TO THE CHURCH has its *Occasion* in ch. iii, it has its *Expression* in ch. iv. 1–22. This passage is in four parts as follows :—

1. THE APPREHENSION (1–4). Three things combined served as occasion for the Apostles' arrest, religious intolerance, political animosity, and rationalistic unbelief. These are represented by the priests, the captain, and the Sadducees (1), and the fact of Christ's resurrection condemned them all (2), as it continuously condemns the corruptions of the Church, the despotism of the world, and the pride of infidelity. And so it was thought best that these men should be " *put inward* " (3). However, you do not

cow the lion by caging it, or break an eagle's spirit by breaking its wing. In spite of all opposition, many will believe (4). The five thousand here referred to, were all *men* (andron), and were in addition to the three thousand on the Day of Pentecost.

2. THE EXAMINATION (5–12). Mark, first of all, (a) *The Council's Inquiry* (5–7). Take a good look at these people : rulers, elders, scribes, Annas, Caiaphas, John, Alexander, many, for what they lacked in weight they made up for by number (5). " *By what power ? or by what name ?* " (7). See ch. iii. 6, 12, 16, and also iv. 12. The emphasis is upon " ye " (Gr.), meaning " such as you " unlearned and contemptible men. That has always been the way with the highbrows, but abuse is never an argument. Contempt is always contemptible, except when we " pour contempt on all our pride." Now mark (b) *The Apostle's Reply* (8—12). Here is first, an affirmation (8–9), and then, an interpretation (10–12) of the miracle-fact. Christ, killed by them, but raised by God, is the sufficient explanation of this man's cure (10). *Builders* should be good judges of *stones*, but, as often, the experts were mistaken (11). But in spite of it all, there is salvation, by a Name, by one Name only, and for all (12). That is the Gospel—*One for all.* This is Peter's *fourth* discourse.

Thought : *CONFIDENCE IN CHRIST BEGETS COURAGE FOR THE CONFLICT.*

THE ACTS iv. 13-22

Title : *THE IMPOTENCE OF THE POWERS*

13 Now when they saw the boldness of Peter and John, and perceived that they were unlearned and ignorant men, they marvelled ; and they took knowledge of them, that they had been with Jesus. 14 And beholding the man which was healed standing with them, they could say nothing against it.

15 But when they had commanded them to go aside out of the council, they conferred among themselves, 16 Saying, What shall we do to these men ? for that indeed a notable miracle hath been done by them is manifest to all them that dwell in Jerusalem ; and we cannot deny it. 17 But that it spread no further among the people, let us straitly threaten them, that they speak henceforth to no man in this name. 18 And they called them, and commanded them not to speak at all nor teach in the name of Jesus.

19 But Peter and John answered and said unto them, Whether it be right in the sight of God to hearken unto you more than unto God, judge ye, 20 For we cannot but speak the things which we have seen and heard. 21 So when they had further threatened them, they let them go, finding nothing how they might punish them, because of the people : for all men glorified God for that which was done. 22 For the man was above forty years old, on whom this miracle of healing was shewed.

EXPOSITION

We come now to—3. THE CONSULTATION (13–17). Peter and John and the healed man are led out to an ante-room, whilst these authorities discuss their case behind closed doors (14, 15). The scene and sound would be laughable if it were not so sad. Here is a crowd of men up against a fact ; " *we cannot deny it*," they say, it is " *indeed a notable miracle*," and " *is manifest to all in Jerusalem* " (16). Very well, what's the difficulty ? The difficulty is this, that they do not wish it to be a fact ! That's awkward ; but facts are stubborn things. So they say, " *What shall we do to these men ?* ", not, " What shall we do with the facts ? " but " How shall we escape dealing fairly with them ? " Think of it ! There you see not only malice, but also cowardice. Infinitely better be *unlearned* and *unschooled* like Peter and John, with their courage, than be learned and schooled like these authorities, with their cowardice (13). It was as evident that they had not " *been with Jesus* " as that these Apostles had. Do we present to all men the indisputable evidences that we are *in the habit of being with Jesus* ? Look now at—

4. THE PROHIBITION (18–22). In secret conclave they have arrived at a course of action (17), and they must see it through with as much dignity as they are capable of carrying, and that was not much. They had not learned that red-tape can never be a substitute for rectitude. Have you ? So Peter and John and the healed man are marched in again (18). They had been having a fine time in the ante-room, a prayer-meeting no doubt. They receive the solemn charge (17, 18). But the Council might as well have told the sun not to shine, and the tides not to move, and the winds not to blow, as to tell these men not to talk about Jesus. The Apostle's answer is magnificent (19, 20). " *Whether it be right,*" should always be our first consideration. " Right " is one of the words we ought to restore to its proper place in our thinking, and what it means, to its rightful place in our practice. Settle every question on principle. " Right is right, if God is God, and right the day must win ; to doubt would be disloyalty, and to falter would be sin."

Thought : THE SECOND STORY OF THE
THREE HEBREWS (*cf. Daniel* iii. 24, 25)

THE ACTS iv. 23-37

Title : FROM THE COURT TO THE CHURCH

23 And being let go, they went to their own company, and reported all that the chief priests and elders had said unto them. 24 And when they heard that, they lifted up their voice to God with one accord, and said, Lord, thou art God, which hast made heaven, and earth, and the sea, and all that in

them is : 25 Who by the mouth of thy servant David
hast said, Why did the heathen rage, and the people
imagine vain things? 26 The kings of the earth
stood up, and the rulers were gathered together
against the Lord, and against his Christ. 27 For of
a truth against thy holy child Jesus, whom thou
hast anointed, both Herod, and Pontius Pilate, with
the Gentiles, and the people of Israel, were gathered
together, 28 For to do whatsoever thy hand and
thy counsel determined before to be done. 29 And
now, Lord, behold their threatenings : and grant
unto thy servants, that with all boldness they may
speak thy word, 30 By stretching forth thine
hand to heal ; and that signs and wonders may be
done by the name of thy holy child Jesus. 31 And
when they had prayed, the place was shaken where
they were assembled together ; and they were all
filled with the Holy Ghost, and they spake the word
of God with boldness.

32 And the multitude of them that believed
were of one heart and of one soul : neither said any
of them that ought of the things which he possessed
was his own ; but they had all things common.
33 And with great power gave the apostles witness
of the resurrection of the Lord Jesus : and great
grace was upon them all. 34 Neither was there
any among them that lacked : for as many as were
possessors of lands or houses sold them, and brought
the prices of the things that were sold, 35 And laid
them down at the apostles' feet : and distribution
was made unto every man according as he had
need. 36 And Joses, who by the apostles was
surnamed Barnabas, (which is, being interpreted,
The son of consolation,) a Levite, and of the country
of Cyprus, 37 Having land, sold it, and brought
the money, and laid it at the apostles' feet.

EXPOSITION

Under OPPOSITION TO THE CHURCH, we have
considered the *Occasion* of it (iii. 1–26), and the
Expression of it (iv. 1–22) ; now observe *The Sequel
to it* (iv. 23–31). The Apostles are " *let go.*" What
now will they do ? " *They went to their own company* "

(23). What did you do when you were " let go " ? or, what would you do if you were " let go " ? that is, how do you and I use our freedom ? There are many " *let go* " crises in life ; when we leave school, and home ; when we get aboard an ocean liner ; when we go to some other land. What do we then ? We have to choose our own company, and we always do so according to what we essentially are. What these men *choose* to do now, Judas *had* to do at last (i. 25). What sort of " *company* " is yours ? In our lesson mark three things :

1. PRAISE (24–28). Verses 25, 26 are from Psalm ii, and probably were *sung*. If so, it is the beginning of singing in the Christian Church. They address *God the Creator* (24), and acknowledge Him to be *the sovereign Ruler* (25–28). He is back alike of nature and history. His eternal decrees, and man's free actions interlock (27, 28). That is a mysterious fact : ponder it. We all have something for which to offer *praise*, and there, like the apostles, we should begin.

But inevitably, the next thing will be—2. PRAYER (29, 30). Having reviewed *the past*, they naturally come to the *present* ; and mark the connection between past and present. What God has done, He can do. From days gone by, we should draw encouragement for the present hour. The apostles point to the danger (29a), confess their need of courage (29b), and ask for vindication (30). Their prayer is brief, but comprehensive.

And now follows—3. POWER (31). " *When they had prayed* " something happened. That is when things do happen, for " more things are wrought by prayer than this world dreams of." Mark carefully the three things which did happen ; first, an earthquake, then, a soul-quake, and finally, a tongue-quake.

Thought : "*ASK AND IT SHALL BE GIVEN YOU.*"

Title : UNITY AND COMMUNITY

1 But a certain man named Ananias, with Sapphira, his wife, sold a possession, 2 And kept back part of the price, his wife also being privy to it, and brought a certain part, and laid it at the apostles' feet. 3 But Peter said, Ananias, why hath Satan filled thine heart to lie to the Holy Ghost, and to keep back part of the price of the land ? 4 Whiles it remained, was it not thine own ? and after it was sold, was it not in thine own power ? why hast thou conceived this thing in thine heart ? thou hast not lied unto men, but unto God. 5 And Ananias hearing these words fell down, and gave up the ghost : and great fear came on all them that heard these things. 6 And the young men arose, wound him up, and carried him out, and buried him.

7 And it was about the space of three hours after, when his wife, not knowing what was done, came in. 8 And Peter answered unto her, Tell me whether ye sold the land for so much ? And she said, Yea, for so much. 9 Then Peter said unto her, How is it that ye have agreed together to tempt the Spirit of the Lord ? behold, the feet of them which have buried thy husband are at the door, and shall carry thee out. 10 Then fell she down straightway at his feet, and yielded up the ghost : and the young men came in, and found her dead, and, carrying her forth, buried her by her husband. 11 And great fear came upon all the church, and upon as many as heard these things.

EXPOSITION

After I. FOUNDING (i. 1 to ii. 13), II. WITNESS (ii. 14–47), and III. OPPOSITION (iii. 1 to iv. 31), comes IV. DISCIPLINE IN THE CHURCH (iv. 32 to v. 16) ; and we should consider : The originating circumstances ; the specific occasion ; and the salutary effect. Look then at :

1. THE ORIGINATING CIRCUMSTANCES OF DISCIPLINE (iv. 32-35). This is a passage which may very easily be misinterpreted and misapplied, and indeed, has been. But there is nothing here comparable to modern communism. The reference, to begin with, is not to the *State*, but to the *Church* ; in the second place, the *social community* was based on, and sprang from, *spiritual unity* ; and once again, quite obviously the measure was *exceptional and transitory* and disappeared within the apostolic age. But the spirit and principle remain. All for each, and each for all, is the ideal of the Heavenly Commonwealth, for such is the Christian Church. Never, when the heart has been open, has the pocket been closed. The great generosity of these Christians issued from their " *great grace* " (33).

2. THE SPECIFIC OCCASION OF DISCIPLINE (iv. 36 to v. 11). Two concrete examples of the working of the above enterprise are now given : that of Barnabas (iv. 36 37) ; and that of Ananias and Sapphira (v.1-11) ; the one for commendation, and the other for condemnation. Study carefully what is said of Barnabas, for we are to hear of him again. He is one of a few who rendered great service to the Church in its formative period. What a contrast we have in Ananias and Sapphira ! Alas, early was darnel sown among the wheat. What was the sin of this man and his wife ? *An acted lie.* They were under no compulsion to sell their property ; and having done so, were under no compulsion to hand over to the church the entire proceeds (4a) ; but when they made out that the part was the whole, they lied to the Holy Spirit (4, 9), being actuated by Satan (3). The conviction of Ananias was expressed by Peter, felt by himself, and confirmed by God. The wife, who helped in the sin, shared in the judgment. We must never suppose that the element of good in our actions can counterbalance the element of evil therein. Be straight. Hate hypocrisy as you should the devil.

Thought : THE GOD OF LOVE IS RIGHTEOUS.

Title : ANGEL-HELP

12 And by the hands of the apostles were many signs and wonders wrought among the people ; (and they were all with one accord in Solomon's porch. 13 And of the rest durst no man join himself to them : but the people magnified them. 14 And believers were the more added to the Lord, multitudes both of men and women.) 15 Insomuch that they brought forth the sick into the streets, and laid them on beds and couches, that at the least the shadow of Peter passing by might overshadow some of them. 16 There came also a multitude out of the cities round about unto Jerusalem, bringing sick folks, and them which were vexed with unclean spirits : and they were healed every one.

17 Then the high priest rose up, and all they that were with him, (which is the sect of the Sadducees,) and were filled with indignation, 18 And laid their hands on the apostles, and put them in the common prison. 19 But the angel of the Lord by night opened the prison doors, and brought them forth, and said, 20 Go, stand and speak in the temple to the people all the words of this life. 21 And when they heard that, they entered into the temple early in the morning, and taught. But the high priest came, and they that were with him, and called the council together, and all the senate of the children of Israel, and sent to the prison to have them brought. 22 But when the officers came, and found them not in the prison, they returned, and told, 23 Saying, The prison truly found we shut with all safety, and the keepers standing without before the doors : but when we had opened, we found no man within. 24 Now when the high priest and the captain of the temple and the chief priests heard these things, they doubted of them whereunto this would grow. 25 Then came one and told them, saying, Behold, the men whom ye put in prison are standing in the temple, and teaching the people. 26 Then went the captain with the officers, and brought them without violence : for

they feared the people, lest they should have been stoned.

EXPOSITION

Observe now—3. THE SALUTARY EFFECT OF DISCIPLINE (12–16). It was twofold, in the main, *arresting* and *advancing* the growth of the Church (13, 14). There are two ways in which a church may grow—*like a building*, by adding stone to stone ; and *like a plant*, by development from the root. The one is an *organization*, and the other is an *organism*. It is never safe to judge of the success of a church by the length of its roll. Subtraction is sometimes strength. Only a pure church is powerful. If Ananias and Sapphira had been allowed to remain, this portion would never have been written, and winter, instead of summer, would have settled down on the Church's life. It is abidingly true that that in the Gospel which attracts some, repels others ; but not on this account should the Church lower her standards, or widen her doors. The outflow of judgment may be a preparation for the inflow of grace. Observe what are the elements which entered into this rich experience in the Church's history : *fear* (11), *harmony* (12b), *reverence* (13b), *faith* (14), and *works* (12a, 15, 16).

Our next division tells of—V. THE TESTING OF THE CHURCH (v. 17–42). Here, let us observe, first 1. *The Detention and Deliverance of the Apostles* (17–26). Prosperity brought persecution, but it is the persecutors who are made to look ridiculous, for the forces are unequal, as they always are when God is on one of the sides. Authority is always weak when it has not moral support, and no amount of gold braid and brass buttons can make up for the want of such support. The apostles were delivered not that they might be *safe*, but that they might be *used* (20). Their commission was to " *speak to the people*," and their message was, " *all the words of this life."* Do not overlook the humour of verse 23. In verse 24 read, *" what this might be,"* instead of, *" whereunto this would grow."*

Thought : IT IS HOPELESS TO FIGHT AGAINST GOD.

THE ACTS v. 27-42

Title : WHEN PAIN IS PLEASANT

27 And when they had brought them, they set them before the council : and the high priest asked them, 28 Saying, Did not we straitly command you that ye should not teach in this name ? and, behold, ye have filled Jerusalem with your doctrine, and intend to bring this man's blood upon us. 29 Then Peter and the other apostles answered and said, We ought to obey God rather than men. 30 The God of our fathers raised up Jesus, whom ye slew and hanged on a tree. 31 Him hath God exalted with his right hand to be a Prince and a Saviour, for to give repentance to Israel, and forgiveness of sins. 32 And we are his witnesses of these things ; and so is also the Holy Ghost, whom God hath given to them that obey him.

33 When they heard that, they were cut to the heart, and took counsel to slay them. 34 Then stood there up one in the council, a Pharisee, named Gamaliel, a doctor of the law, had in reputation among all the people, and commanded to put the apostles forth a little space ; 35 And said unto them, Ye men of Israel, take heed to yourselves what ye intend to do as touching these men. 36 For before these days rose up Theudas, boasting himself to be somebody ; to whom a number of men, about four hundred, joined themselves : who was slain ; and all, as many as obeyed him, were scattered, and brought to nought. 37 After this man rose up Judas of Galilee in the days of the taxing, and drew away much people after him : he also perished ; and all, even as many as obeyed him, were dispersed. 38 And now I say unto you, Refrain from

these men, and let them alone : for if this counsel or this work be of men, it will come to nought : 39 But if it be of God, ye cannot overthrow it ; lest haply ye be found even to fight against God.

40 And to him they agreed : and when they had called the apostles, and beaten them, they commanded that they should not speak in the name of Jesus, and let them go. 41 And they departed from the presence of the council, rejoicing that they were counted worthy to suffer shame for his name. 42 And daily in the temple, and in every house, they ceased not to teach and preach Jesus Christ.

EXPOSITION

This portion tells of—2. *The Trial and Triumph of the Apostles* (27–42). Consider,

(a) WHAT THE SANHEDRIN SAID TO THE APOSTLES (27, 28). "*Did we not charge you by a charge ?*" Certainly. "*Ye have filled Jerusalem with your doctrine.*" Well done ; and the sufficient explanation and warrant are to be found in "*this man*," "*this name*," "*this life*," "*this counsel*," and "*this work*" (28, 20, 38). Charging with charges is of no use here.

(b) WHAT THE APOSTLES SAID TO THE SANHEDRIN (29–32). Both times the highest note was struck : "*Whether it be right*," in iv. 19 ; and "*we ought*," here. He is lost who in such a crisis as this consults his comfort or convenience, but he is saved who does his duty. The one only true determining principle for us all is, GOD FIRST. Let us ever do what we *ought* to do in the face of fear, envy, and hate. The apostolic gospel has for its foci the *Cross* and the *Crown*, on the one part, and *repentance* and *remission* on the other part (30, 31). "*We are His witnesses of these things.*" Are we ? The Holy Spirit is (32). "*When they heard, they were saved through*" (33). Resist the truth and it will cut you ; yield to it and it will crown you.

(c) WHAT GAMALIEL SAID TO THEM ALL (34–39). This man was Paul's teacher, and, no doubt greatly influenced him. His speech is a model of its kind, and contains much shrewd common sense. We may learn from him—that there is always danger in repression ; that time is required for the true nature of a movement to be clearly seen ; that movements which have no spiritual vitality in them come to an end, sooner or later, if left alone ; that the past has much to teach the present ; and that it is useless to antagonise the truth. These are great lessons. Three possible attitudes towards God are here in view—*hostility*, " fight against God " ; *neutrality*, " let these men alone " ; and *co-operation*, " teaching and preaching Jesus Christ " (39, 38, 42). How much do we know of joy in the fellowship of shame ? (41).

Thought : THERE IS NO ENTERPRISE WHERE THERE IS NO ENTHUSIASM.

THE ACTS vi. 1-15

Title : GOING AND GROWING

1 And in those days, when the number of the disciples was multiplied, there arose a murmuring of the Grecians against the Hebrews, because their widows were neglected in the daily ministration. 2 Then the twelve called the multitude of the disciples unto them, and said, It is not reason that we should leave the word of God, and serve tables. 3 Wherefore, brethren, look ye out among you seven men of honest report, full of the Holy Ghost and wisdom, whom we may appoint over this business. 4 But we will give ourselves continually to prayer, and to the ministry of the word. 5 And the saying pleased the whole multitude : and they chose Stephen, a man full of faith and of the Holy Ghost, and Philip, and Prochorus, and Nicanor, and Timon, and Parmenas, and Nicolas a proselyte of Antioch : 6 Whom they set before the apostles : and when they had prayed, they laid their hands on them.

7 And the word of God increased; and the number of the disciples multiplied in Jerusalem greatly; and a great company of the priests were obedient to the faith.

8 And Stephen, full of faith and power, did great wonders and miracles among the people. 9 Then there arose certain of the synagogue, which is called the synagogue of the Libertines, and Cyrenians, and Alexandrians, and of them of Cilicia and of Asia, disputing with Stephen. 10 And they were not able to resist the wisdom and the spirit by which he spake. 11 Then they suborned men, which said, We have heard him speak blasphemous words against Moses, and against God. 12 And they stirred up the people, and the elders, and the scribes, and came upon him, and caught him, and brought him to the council, 13 And set up false witnesses, which said, This man ceaseth not to speak blasphemous words against this holy place, and the law : 14 For we have heard him say, that this Jesus of Nazareth shall destroy this place, and shall change the customs which Moses delivered us. 15 And all that sat in the council, looking stedfastly on him, saw his face as it had been the face of an angel.

EXPOSITION

The next development in this story is—VI. ADMINISTRATION IN THE CHURCH (1–6). We should mark first of all, 1. *The Complaint of the Disciples* (1). One of the earliest Christian institutions was *an order of widows*, who were maintained at the common cost, and who gave themselves to prayer and works of mercy (ix. 41 ; 1 Tim. v. 3, 9, 10, 11, 16). Greek-speaking Jews here complain against Aramaic-speaking Jews, declaring that the fund was not being fairly administered. What a lot of murmuring there has been over money ! Of course, Church funds should be properly used, and all complaint is not contrariety.

2. *The Conference of the Church* (2–4). This is the first Church Business Meeting on record, and it was " proposed and carried " that a new

office be created to handle the " temporalities " of the Church, so that the apostles might continue to care for the " spiritualities " (2, 4). The procedure was thoroughly democratic. *Deacons* are now appointed (3, 1 Tim. iii. 8–13). Co-operation by distribution of labour is a fundamental principle of success, in the Church, and out of it. The supreme work of the minister is defined in verse 4 : supplication in private, and ministration in public, and always in that order ; to these, such should " *give themselves.*" 3. *The Choice of Deacons* (5, 6). It is worth while to observe, in the light of complaint (1), that they all bear Greek names (5). What qualifications are required of a Church deacon ? He must be reputable, wise, and Spirit-filled (3). Do all deacons foot that line ? The chosen are then consecrated (6) ; and the Church continues to prosper (7).

We now come to the last section in the first division of the Book.

VII. PERSECUTION OF THE CHURCH (vi. 7 to viii. 4). Mark carefully, the reason, focus, and result of it. 1. *The Reason of it* is the rapid growth of the Church (7). Decaying institutions are always jealous of new and vigorous enterprises. 2. *The Focus of it* (ver. 8 to ch. viii. 1a). STEPHEN. What a contrast is here presented ! Faithfulness and fanaticism, power and weakness, truth and error, deeds and lies, one and many ! Resort to physical force is never an argument in the realm of the spiritual. Truth is never hysterical. Reality is ever sovereign.

Thought : *EVERY CHRISTIAN IS CALLED TO WORK AND WITNESS.*

THE ACTS vii. 1-16

Title : A GREAT SERMON

1 Then said the high priest, Are these things so ? 2 And he said, Men, brethren, and fathers, hearken ; The God of glory appeared unto our

father Abraham, when he was in Mesopotamia, before he dwelt in Charran, 3 And said unto him, Get thee out of thy country, and from thy kindred, and come into the land which I shall shew thee. 4 Then came he out of the land of the Chaldæans, and dwelt in Charran : and from thence, when his father was dead, he removed him unto this land, wherein ye now dwell. 5 And he gave him none inheritance in it, no, not so much as to set his foot on : yet he promised that he would give it to him for a possession, and to his seed after him, when as yet he had no child.

6 And God spake on this wise, That his seed should sojourn in a strange land ; and that they should bring them into bondage, and entreat them evil four hundred years. 7 And the nation to whom they shall be in bondage will I judge, said God : and after that shall they come forth, and serve me in this place. 8 And he gave him the covenant of circumcision : and so Abraham begat Isaac, and circumcised him the eighth day ; and Isaac begat Jacob ; and Jacob begat the twelve patriarchs. 9 And the patriarchs, moved with envy, sold Joseph into Egypt : but God was with him. 10 And delivered him out of all his afflictions, and gave him favour and wisdom in the sight of Pharaoh king of Egypt ; and he made him governor over Egypt and all his house.

11 Now there came a dearth over all the land of Egypt and Chanaan, and great affliction : and our fathers found no sustenance. 12 But when Jacob heard that there was corn in Egypt, he sent out our fathers first. 13 And at the second time Joseph was made known to his brethren ; and Joseph's kindred was made known unto Pharaoh. 14 Then sent Joseph, and called his father Jacob to him, and all his kindred, threescore and fifteen souls. 15 So Jacob went down into Egypt, and died, he, and our fathers. 16 And were carried over into Sychem, and laid in the sepulchre that Abraham bought for a sum of money of the sons of Emmor the father of Sychem.

EXPOSITION.

We are still considering STEPHEN as *the Focus of Persecution*. The brunt of the battle falls upon its leaders ; it is the front line that feels the full force of the attack. I doubt not the other six deacons were quite loyal, but it is Stephen who draws the enemy (vi. 8, 9). Having been charged (vi. 13, 14), he is now put on his defence (vii. 1). How does he reply ? By reviewing the history of his people (2–50). But is that a reply ? Yes, rightly understood it is, for the true view of Jesus and His mission rests on the whole past history of the Hebrew people. Divine revelation is progressive, and it was fatal not to follow until it was consummated in the life and sacrifice of Christ. The Jews have been left behind because they did not follow in that greatest crisis of human history.

A word first of all about (a) *The Preacher*. We cannot but be impressed by his fearlessness of man, his courage born of deep conviction, his freedom from Jewish prejudice, and his knowledge of the Scriptures ; also his skill in argument, rhetorical power, spiritual insight, and self-command. Next, survey (b) *The Sermon*. In scope it reaches from ABRAHAM to SOLOMON (2, 47), and here the history is followed chronologically, those events in it being selected which best served the purpose of Stephen's defence. The two main divisions are—(a) THE HEBREW FAMILY (2–16), and (b) THE ISRAELITISH NATION (17–50). The first of these covers Genesis xi. to l. Two figures stand out in the scene. ABRAHAM, the father of the Hebrews (2–8), and JOSEPH, the saviour of his people (9–16). The former illustrates *the Divine election*, and the latter, *the Divine providence*. Both these run all through history, and give to it its real significance and worth ; for what matters in history is what God is doing in it. " Through the ages one increasing purpose runs." In heaven's light much success is seen to be failure, and much failure is seen to be success.

Thought : *LEARN HOW TO USE YOUR*
            BIBLE

Title : FROM THE COURT TO THE DESERT

17 But when the time of the promise drew nigh, which God had sworn to Abraham, the people grew and multiplied in Egypt, 18 Till another king arose, which knew not Joseph. 19 The same dealt subtilly with our kindred, and evil entreated our fathers, so that they cast out their young children, to the end they might not live. 20 In which time Moses was born, and was exceeding fair, and nourished up in his father's house three months : 21 And when he was cast out, Pharaoh's daughter took him up, and nourished him for her own son. 22 And Moses was learned in all the wisdom of the Egyptians, and was mighty in words and in deeds. 23 And when he was full forty years old, it came into his heart to visit his brethren the children of Israel. 24 And seeing one of them suffer wrong, he defended him, and avenged him that was oppressed, and smote the Egyptian : 25 For he supposed his brethren would have understood how that God by his hand would deliver them : but they understood not. 26 And the next day he shewed himself unto them as they strove, and would have set them at one again, saying, Sirs, ye are brethren ; why do ye wrong one to another ? 27 But he that did his neighbour wrong thrust him away, saying, Who made thee a ruler and a judge over us ? 28 Wilt thou kill me, as thou diddest the Egyptian yesterday ? 29 Then fled Moses at this saying, and was a stranger in the land of Madian, where he begat two sons.

EXPOSITION

The second main part of this sermon is a review of (b) THE ISRAELITISH NATION (17–50) in two great periods of its history, the Theocracy, and the Monarchy. Look at these.

1. THE THEOCRACY (17–45). The line followed is chronological, geographical and biographical. If in the previous part, ABRAHAM and JOSEPH dominate, here, MOSES dominates.

Attention is first called to, (i) *Israel in Egypt* (17–36). Our portion takes the story up to the end of Moses' sojourn in Midian, embracing eighty years of his life. A number of important truths and lessons crowd in here ; among which observe that God's promise is His purpose, and it is never lost sight of (17) ; that struggles always precede freedom ; permanent good must sooner or later be struggled for (18, 19) ; that in the hour of our greatest need, God draws near to help us, in some way or through some one : when the hour comes the man is not wanting, and no movement is ripe until the leader appears (20) ; that those whom God would use, He carefully prepares (20–22) ; that an insignificant event may at any time precipitate a momentous crisis (24) ; a trifling circumstance may stimulate to energetic action : thus, the act of Moses in delivering the individual Israelite from his oppressor greatly promoted his national design. " Do the thing that lies nearest to thee ; the second will have already become clearer."

A further lesson is, that we must remain true to the highest we know, though we be misunderstood (25). Read, " *Now he supposed his brethren would understand how that God, by his hand is giving them salvation : but they understood not.*" If we are in the way of God's will, we must not allow misunderstanding, on the part of foe or friend, to chill our enthusiasm, or arrest our endeavour. Better be an exile for the truth than a craven at home (29). Oh, these misunderstandings among brethren ! They need not be. Is there anything of the kind which you can straighten out to-day ?

Thought : SUFFERING IS THE PRICE OF LEADERSHIP.

THE ACTS vii. 30-43

Title : FETTERS BROKEN AND REFORGED

30 And when forty years were expired, there appeared to him in the wilderness of mount Sina

an angel of the Lord in a flame of fire in a bush. 31 When Moses saw it, he wondered at the sight : and as he drew near to behold it, the voice of the Lord came unto him, 32 Saying, I am the God of thy fathers, the God of Abraham, and the God of Isaac, and the God of Jacob. Then Moses trembled, and durst not behold. 33 Then said the Lord to him, Put off thy shoes from thy feet : for the place where thou standest is holy ground. 34 I have seen, I have seen the affliction of my people which is in Egypt, and I have heard their groaning, and am come down to deliver them. And now come, I will send thee into Egypt.

35 This Moses whom they refused, saying, Who made thee a ruler and a judge ? the same did God send to be a ruler and a deliverer by the hand of the angel which appeared to him in the bush. 36 He brought them out, after that he had shewed wonders and signs in the land of Egypt, and in the Red sea, and in the wilderness forty years. 37 This is that Moses, which said unto the children of Israel, A prophet shall the Lord your God raise up unto you of your brethren, like unto me ; him shall ye hear. 38 This is he that was in the church in the wilderness with the angel which spake to him in the mount Sina, and with our fathers : who received the lively oracles to give unto us : 39 To whom our fathers would not obey, but thrust him from them, and in their hearts turned back again into Egypt. 40 Saying unto Aaron, Make us gods to go before us : for as for this Moses, which brought us out of the land of Egypt, we wot not what is become of him.

41 And they made a calf in those days, and offered sacrifice unto the idol, and rejoiced in the works of their own hands. 42 Then God turned, and gave them up to worship the host of heaven ; as it is written in the book of the prophets, O ye house of Israel, have ye offered to me slain beasts and sacrifices by the space of forty years in the wilderness ? 43 Yea, ye took up the tabernacle of Moloch, and the star of your god Remphan, figures which ye made to worship them ; and I will carry you away beyond Babylon.

EXPOSITION

Stephen is still speaking about (i) *Israel in Egypt* (17–36). Moses was for forty years in the Egyptian Court (20–28) ; for forty years in Midian (29, 30a) ; and now he enters upon the third period of forty years (36, 42). In these periods respectively, he was Prince, Pastor, and Prophet ; first, learning that he was somebody ; then, that he was nobody ; and finally that God was All. Verses 30–34 tell of the *Call of Moses* to accomplish that for which he had been preparing for eighty years. Youth is in too much of a hurry, and generally is impatient of training days. Remember Moses : and also, that for three and a half years' service, Christ had over thirty years of preparation. Training days are tremendous days, and once past they do not come again ; so be patient and diligent.

Before Moses saw the *vision*, and heard the *voice* (30, 31), God saw a *vision*, and heard a *voice* (34). He always sees and hears before we do ; and we see and hear only because He does. Note this also : He says, " *I am come . . . come thou* " (34). He Himself does what He sends us to do (34). " *I will send thee into Egypt* " (34), that is, to the place where our task begins. He sends, but we must go. The next scene is :

(ii) *Israel in the Wilderness* (36–43). Stephen's point here is, though he does not plainly say so, that the people to whom he is speaking are now rejecting the Messiah as their forebears had rejected Moses. " *Like unto me* " (37). How ? Each had a special preparation ; each had a Divine call ; each founded a dispensation ; each was a new spiritual force, each was a great religious teacher ; each claimed a hearing on Divine authority ; and each was rejected by his own generation. But Messiah was greater than Moses. Much in this review is passed over by Stephen, but he fixed on Israel's idolatry (39–43), the sin which brought them into a new captivity ; for observe that after *exit from Egypt* (36), is *entrance into Babylon* (43). Let the delivered beware of further bondage.

Thought : OUR FREEDOM IS HIS GRAND CONTROL.

THE ACTS vii. 44-60

Title : THE FIRST CHRISTIAN MARTYR

44 Our fathers had the tabernacle of witness in the wilderness, as he had appointed, speaking unto Moses, that he should make it according to the fashion that he had seen. 45 Which also our fathers that came after brought in with Jesus into the possession of the Gentiles, whom God drave out before the face of our fathers, unto the days of David ; 46 Who found favour before God, and desired to find a tabernacle for the God of Jacob. 47 But Solomon built him an house. 48 Howbeit the most High dwelleth not in temples made with hands ; as saith the prophet, 49 Heaven is my throne, and earth is my footstool : what house will ye build me ? saith the Lord : or what is the place of my rest ? 50 Hath not my hand made all these things ?

51 Ye stiffnecked and uncircumcised in heart and ears, ye do always resist the Holy Ghost : as your fathers did, so do ye. 52 Which of the prophets have not your fathers persecuted ? and they have slain them which shewed before of the coming of the Just One ; of whom ye have been now the betrayers and murderers : 53 Who have received the law by the disposition of angels, and have not kept it.

54 When they heard these things, they were cut to the heart, and they gnashed on him with their teeth. 55 But he, being full of the Holy Ghost, looked up stedfastly into heaven, and saw the glory of God, and Jesus standing on the right hand of God. 56 And said, Behold, I see the heavens opened, and the Son of man standing on the right hand of God. 57 Then they cried out with a loud voice, and

stopped their ears, and ran upon him with one
accord, 58 And cast him out of the city, and stoned
him : and the witnesses laid down their clothes at
a young man's feet, whose name was Saul. 59 And
they stoned Stephen, calling upon God, and saying,
Lord Jesus, receive my spirit. 60 And he kneeled
down, and cried with a loud voice, Lord, lay not
this sin to their charge. And when he had said
this, he fell asleep.

EXPOSITION

In the period of THE THEOCRACY in this Sermon,
Stephen has told the story of Israel in Egypt, and in
the Wilderness ; now we are given a glimpse of :

(iii) *Israel in the Land* (44–50). This is sketched
very briefly, reference being made only to JOSHUA,
and, in the period of THE MONARCHY, to DAVID and
SOLOMON. Part of the charge brought against
Stephen was that he spake " *blasphemous words against
this holy place* " (13, 14) ; now he replies to that,
passing from the *Tabernacle* (44) through the *Temple*
(47) to the *Universe* (49, 50). At this point, it would
appear, he was interrupted by a hostile crowd, and
he turns from his survey to characterize and charge
these people (51–53). Stephen was the most gracious
of men, but he could speak words which bit and
burned. In both these respects he was like his
Master (cf. 51, 60). What a picture of moral depravity
verses 54, 57, 58, present ! And what a picture of
moral and spiritual nobility verses 59, 60 present !
In Stephen's hour of anguish he was vouchsafed a
vision : " *Jesus standing* " (55). Compare Hebrews x.
12. Did He *rise* to welcome the first Christian
martyr ? How often in the history of God's people
suffering and sight have gone together ! How stupid
and useless a thing it is for men to persecute those
who do not think and act as they do. Stephen could
be got rid of by means of stones ; but not the Truth.
Here that saying has its first illustration, that " *the
blood of the martyrs is the seed of the Church.*"

Saul saw Stephen die, after having heard him preach, and, I doubt not, Stephen is Saul's spiritual father ; the sacrifice of the one led to the salvation of the other. See how a Christian can die (59, 60) ! Only a godlike soul can pray as Stephen did. Compare Samson's prayer in Judges xvi. 28. Compare also, " *With one accord* " (57), with ii. 1. Is your agreement with heaven, or with hell ?

Thought : *PRECIOUS IN GOD'S SIGHT IS THE DEATH OF HIS SAINTS.*

THE ACTS viii. 1-13

Title : PHILIP AT SAMARIA

1 And Saul was consenting unto his death. And at that time there was a great persecution against the church which was at Jerusalem ; and they were all scattered abroad throughout the regions of Judæa and Samaria, except the apostles. 2 And devout men carried Stephen to his burial, and made great lamentation over him. 3 As for Saul, he made havoc of the church, entering into every house, and haling men and women committed them to prison.

4 Therefore they that were scattered abroad went every where preaching the word. 5 Then Philip went down to the city of Samaria, and preached Christ unto them. 6 And the people with one accord gave heed unto those things which Philip spake, hearing and seeing the miracles which he did. 7 For unclean spirits, crying with loud voice, came out of many that were possessed with them : and many taken with palsies, and that were lame, were healed. 8 And there was great joy in that city.

9 But there was a certain man, called Simon, which beforetime in the same city used sorcery, and bewitched the people of Samaria, giving out that himself was some great one : 10 To whom they all gave heed, from the least to the greatest,

65

saying, This man is the great power of God. 11 And to him they had regard, because that of long time he had bewitched them with sorceries. 12 But when they believed Philip preaching the things concerning the kingdom of God, and the name of Jesus Christ, they were baptized, both men and women. 13 Then Simon himself believed also : and when he was baptized, he continued with Philip, and wondered, beholding the miracles and signs which were done.

EXPOSITION

We now come to the end of THE JEWISH PERIOD OF THE CHURCH'S WITNESS (i. 1 to viii. 4), having followed the Founding, Witness, Opposition, Discipline, Testing, Administration, and Persecution of the Church. That which has been FOUNDED, is now BROADENED in what, let us call, THE TRANSITION PERIOD OF THE CHURCH'S WITNESS (viii. 5 to xii. 25). Period one covers A.D. 30-35. Period two covers A.D. 35-44. Here there are five main sections. Before entering upon these let us glance at the concluding section of the first main division (viii. 1-4). This tells us that Stephen was buried and greatly mourned ; that from the Stephen centre of suffering was described a wide circumference of persecution ; that, in consequence, the Jerusalem Christians were scattered abroad, and that the scattering was as seed which was to produce a great and golden harvest. It ever has been so. The devil's breath has fanned the flames of the Gospel. The bruised tree has filled the air with perfume.

Coming now to the second main division of this Book, we have first of all—1. PHILIP'S PREPARATION FOR THE WIDER WITNESS (viii. 5-40). Here we are told of :

(i) THE GOSPEL AT SAMARIA (5-25), and first, (a) *Under Philip* (5-13). This is not the Apostle, but Philip the *deacon* (vi. 5), and *evangelist* (xxi. 8). How was it that he met with such good success at Samaria ? Read John iv. 39-42. A woman sows, and a man reaps ; and the reaper himself becomes a sower for other reapers. No one can fail who goes forth with Philip's message (5), and this great message believed, is productive of *great joy* (8). " *But*," yes, there is always a " *but* " (9) : some fly in the ointment ; some drag on the wheel. Here is Christianity's first collision with sorcery and superstition (9–13), and Christianity won. So far from the sheep being devoured by the wolf, the wolf aped the sheep. Simon was a humbug. Make quite sure that you are not.

Thought : *IN EVERY GOOD WORK THERE ARE DISAPPOINTMENTS.*

THE ACTS viii. 14-25

Title : *SIMON THE SORCERER*

14 Now when the apostles which were at Jerusalem heard that Samaria had received the word of God, they sent unto them Peter and John : **15** Who, when they were come down, prayed for them, that they might receive the Holy Ghost : **16** (For as yet he was fallen upon none of them : only they were baptized in the name of the Lord Jesus.) **17** Then laid they their hands on them, and they received the Holy Ghost. **18** And when Simon saw that through laying on of the apostles' hands the Holy Ghost was given, he offered them money, **19** Saying, Give me also this power, that on whomsoever I lay hands, he may receive the Holy Ghost. **20** But Peter said unto him, Thy money perish with thee, because thou hast thought that the gift of God may be purchased with money. **21** Thou hast neither part nor lot in this matter : for thy heart is not right in the sight of God. **22** Repent therefore of this thy wickedness, and pray God, if perhaps the thought of thine heart may be forgiven thee. **23** For I perceive that thou art in the gall of bitterness, and in the bond of iniquity.

24 Then answered Simon, and said, Pray ye to the Lord for me, that none of these things which ye have spoken come upon me.

25 And they, when they had testified and preached the word of the Lord, returned to Jerusalem, and preached the gospel in many villages of the Samaritans.

EXPOSITION

The Gospel at Samaria—(b) *Under the Apostles* (14–25). We should remember as we read the Acts, that in this record one dispensation is ending, and another is beginning : Judaism is passing, and Christianity is dawning. This means that, as in all transition periods, there necessarily are factors and features which, as to their particular manner and manifestation, are transitory and not permanent. An illustration of this is in our portion (15–17). In one sense every one, in the hour of his regeneration, receives the Holy Spirit. In another sense, in the hour of one's deliberate and full consecration to God, he appropriates the Divine Gift ; but there is *now* no such communication of the Spirit as there was at Samaria. Modes, methods, and manners change, but spiritual realities remain.

And now we meet SIMON again (18–24). What before (13) seemed to be a great triumph, is here seen to have been a veritable tragedy : the believer is found to be a blasphemer. " *He offered them money* " (18). There have not been wanting in the church since then, those who would have taken it, but they could not have " delivered the goods." This unenviable man has left a mark on literature, and on ecclesiasticism. Shakespeare uses his name in the line, " Simony was fair play " ; and in the Church, simony is the act, practice, or crime of trafficking in sacred things, and especially in the buying and selling of ecclesiastical preferments, of the corrupt presentation of any one to an ecclesiastical benefice for money or reward. " But," says Blackstone, " the law has established so many exceptions that there is no difficulty whatever in avoiding the forfeiture," which is imposed for such practice. But there are some things which, though they may be imitated, cannot be counterfeited, and foremost of these is *the power of the Holy Spirit.* Fleshly energy can pass for spiritual power only among those who are wholly lacking in discernment. You ask—but was not Simon truly saved ? (13). Certainly not (21–23). Every professor is not a possessor ; every Church member is not a Christian ; every communicant is not " born again." Are you ? Hypocrites should be spoken to as Peter spoke to Simon. Such, are not occasions for " bated breath, and whispering humbleness," but for courage and firmness, not unmingled with hope (22).

Thought : *PRETENCE CAN NEVER PASS FOR POWER.*

THE ACTS viii. 26-40

Title : *EUNUCH AND EVANGELIST CONFER*

26 And the angel of the Lord spake unto Philip, saying, Arise, and go toward the south unto the way that goeth down from Jerusalem unto Gaza, which is desert. 27 And he arose and went : and, behold, a man of Ethiopia, an eunuch of great authority under Candace queen of the Ethiopians, who had the charge of all her treasure, and had come to Jerusalem for to worship, 28 Was returning, and sitting in his chariot read Esaias the prophet. 29 Then the Spirit said unto Philip, Go near, and join thyself to this chariot. 30 And Philip ran thither to him, and heard him read the prophet Esaias, and said, Understandest thou what thou readest ? 31 And he said, How can I, except some man should guide me ? And he desired Philip that he would come up and sit with him.

32 The place of the scripture which he read was this, He was led as a sheep to the slaughter ; and like a lamb dumb before his shearer, so opened he not his mouth : 33 In his humiliation his judgment

was taken away : and who shall declare his generation ? for his life is taken from the earth.

34 And the eunuch answered Philip, and said,
I pray thee, of whom speaketh the prophet this ? of
himself, or of some other man ? 35 Then Philip
opened his mouth, and began at the same scripture,
and preached unto him Jesus. 36 And as they went
on their way, they came unto a certain water : and
the eunuch said, See, here is water ; what doth
hinder me to be baptized ? 37 And Philip said, If
thou believest with all thine heart, thou mayest.
And he answered and said, I believe that Jesus Christ
is the Son of God. 38 And he commanded the
chariot to stand still : and they went down both into
the water, both Philip and the eunuch ; and he
baptized him. 39 And when they were come up
out of the water, the Spirit of the Lord caught away
Philip that the eunuch saw him no more : and he
went on his way rejoicing. 40 But Philip was
found at Azotus : and passing through he preached
in all the cities, till he came to Cæsarea.

EXPOSITION

Attention has been called to—(i) THE GOSPEL AT
SAMARIA (5–25) ; now it is called to :

(ii) THE GOSPEL TOWARDS AFRICA (26–40) ; and
with this ends Philip's preparation for the wider
witness. Our portion is full of interest. A man in
the midst of a flourishing mission in a city is commanded to leave it, and go to a desert to talk to a
single soul. Was that worth while ? The Lord
thought so (26), and so it proved to be, for by leaving
the city he reached a continent ; through the eunuch
Philip gave the Gospel to Africa. Was it worth while
for a simple unknown preacher to have delivered his
brief message in a little chapel in an English village
one snowy day ? A thousand times worth while, for
there and then Charles Haddon Spurgeon was saved,
and he became the greatest Gospel preacher of the
Christian Age. May the Lord deliver us from
counting heads ; from measuring success by the
arithmetic table. The Lord said, " *arise and go.*"

Philip "*arose and went.*" No one who acts thus, is unblessed.

Now look at this eunuch. We see first, (1) *A Dissatisfied Man* (27), notwithstanding that he had position, power, and possessions. Then, we see, (b) *An Enquiring Man* (28–35), diligent, humble and teachable. And finally, we see (c) *A Converted Man* (36, 38, 39 : verse 37, not in R.V.) believing, confessing, and rejoicing. There, in that chariot, are a high official of an African Royal Court, and a simple evangelist of the Jerusalem Church, the one reading, and the other explaining Isaiah liii. It is clear that Philip did not regard the suffering servant of this Old Testament chapter, to be Israel, but Jesus (35). There is a scholarship in insight we are too apt to overlook, or to despise. I wonder, what the eunuch said to the Queen when he got back ! I wonder what Philip would say if he could see missions in Africa to-day ! Perhaps he can.

Thought : CHRISTIANITY DISCOVERED AND DISCLOSED THE WORTH OF THE INDIVIDUAL SOUL.

THE ACTS ix. 1-16

Title : SAUL'S CONVERSION

1 And Saul, yet breathing out threatenings and slaughter against the disciples of the Lord, went unto the high priest, 2 And desired of him letters to Damascus to the synagogues, that if he found any of this way, whether they were men or women, he might bring them bound unto Jerusalem.

3 And as he journeyed, he came near Damascus : and suddenly there shined round about him a light from heaven : 4 And he fell to the earth, and heard a voice saying unto him, Saul, Saul, why persecutest thou me ? 5 And he said, Who art thou, Lord ? And the Lord said, I am Jesus whom thou

persecutest : it is hard for thee to kick against the pricks. 6 And he trembling and astonished said, Lord, what wilt thou have me to do ? And the Lord said unto him, Arise, and go into the city, and it shall be told thee what thou must do. 7 And the men which journeyed with him stood speechless, hearing a voice, but seeing no man. 8 And Saul arose from the earth ; and when his eyes were opened, he saw no man : but they led him by the hand, and brought him unto Damascus. 9 And he was three days without sight, and neither did eat nor drink.

10 And there was a certain disciple at Damascus, named Ananias ; and to him said the Lord in a vision, Ananias. And he said, Behold, I am here, Lord. 11 And the Lord said unto him, Arise, and go into the street which is called Straight, and enquire in the house of Judas for one called Saul, of Tarsus : for, behold, he prayeth, 12 And hath seen in a vision a man named Ananias coming in, and putting his hand on him, that he might receive his sight. 13 Then Ananias answered, Lord, I have heard by many of this man, how much evil he hath done to thy saints at Jerusalem : 14 And here he hath authority from the chief priests to bind all that call on thy name. 15 But the Lord said unto him, Go thy way : for he is a chosen vessel unto me, to bear my name before the Gentiles, and kings, and the children of Israel : 16 For I will shew him how great things he must suffer for my name's sake.

EXPOSITION

This chapter presents—2. SAUL'S PREPARATION FOR THE WIDER WITNESS (1–31). Here are, conversion, consecration, confession, and conspiracy.

(i) *The Conversion of Saul* (1–9). Of all the remarkable events in the history of the soul, probably the most remarkable is the conversion of Paul, the memory of which is continuously celebrated on the 25th of January. This most remarkable event is recorded three times, here, in xxii. 4–11 ; and in xxvi. 9–18. We are shown how the ravenous wolf became a great sheep-dog ; how the fierce persecutor became the foremost preacher.

What made Saul so fierce ? Stephen's sermon. Never is a man madly irritated against an opinion, violent against a cause or a person, but it is a symptom of a struggle within. The man is really at war with himself. A conviction is reluctantly forcing its way upon him ; he feels the goads of conscience, and vents his resentment upon objects outside of himself. Have you not felt like that ?

Who was he so mad against ? The people of *the Way* (2). This was the earliest name for what we now call Christianity ; and very significant it is, for Christianity is a way of thinking, of feeling, of living, and of serving. Well, Christ apprehended the man who was out to apprehend the Christians (i. 2, Phil. iii. 12). It was all very sudden.

> " Between the stirrup and the ground,
>   He mercy sought, and mercy found."

Omit in verses 5, 6, from " *it is hard* " to " *unto him* " (R.V.). The two great questions for us all, are " *Who ?* " and " *what ?* " (5, 6), the one of doctrine, and the other of duty.

(ii) *The Consecration of Saul* (10–19). Study carefully this new personality, Ananias, and also, what he is told about Saul. The blind man goes into retreat to see more clearly his Saviour (9). There he prays (11), and prepares for the future (15, 16), to do, and to endure. Which is the harder ?

*Thought : ABLE TO SAVE TO THE UTTER-
        MOST.*

THE ACTS ix. 17-31

Title : A NEW PREACHER

17 And Ananias went his way, and entered into the house ; and putting his hands on him said, Brother Saul, the Lord, even Jesus, that appeared unto thee in the way as thou camest, hath sent me,

that thou mightest receive thy sight, and be filled with the Holy Ghost. 18 And immediately there fell from his eyes as it had been scales : and he received sight forthwith, and arose, and was baptized. 19 And when he had received meat, he was strengthened.

Then was Saul certain days with the disciples which were at Damascus. 20 And straightway he preached Christ in the synagogues, that he is the Son of God. 21 But all that heard him were amazed, and said ; Is not this he that destroyed them which called on this name in Jerusalem, and came hither for that intent, that he might bring them bound unto the chief priests ? 22 But Saul increased the more in strength, and confounded the Jews which dwelt at Damascus, proving that this is very Christ.

23 And after that many days were fulfilled, the Jews took counsel to kill him : 24 But their laying await was known of Saul. And they watched the gates day and night to kill him. 25 Then the disciples took him by night, and let him down by the wall in a basket.

26 And when Saul was come to Jerusalem, he assayed to join himself to the disciples : but they were all afraid of him, and believed not that he was a disciple. 27 But Barnabas took him, and brought him to the apostles, and declared unto them how he had seen the Lord in the way, and that he had spoken to him, and how he had preached boldly at Damascus in the name of Jesus. 28 And he was with them coming in and going out at Jerusalem. 29 And he spake boldly in the name of the Lord Jesus, and disputed against the Grecians : but they went about to slay him. 30 Which when the brethren knew, they brought him down to Cæsarea, and sent him forth to Tarsus. 31 Then had the churches rest throughout all Judæa and Galilee and Samaria, and were edified ; and walking in the fear of the Lord, and in the comfort of the Holy Ghost, were multiplied.

EXPOSITION

We are still considering PAUL'S PREPARATION FOR THE WIDER WITNESS. Having regarded his *Conver-*

sion (1–9), and *Consecration* (10–19a), attention is now called to :

(iii) *The Confession of Saul* (19b–22). How bold and blessed it was. A point of chronology is of great interest and importance here. From Galatians i. 17, 18, we learn that Saul went into retreat in Arabia at this time, which event we must place between verses 19, 20, or verses 22, 23, or verses 25, 26, of our lesson : if after verse 22, " *many days* " (23) would point to these years. Saul's conversion was so astounding an experience that he needed time to get the new perspective of his life and thought. During that three years he would read the Old Testament again, and understand it as he never had done before. With every new spiritual experience, we come into possession of a more wonderful Bible.

Little did Saul imagine that he was to become the Church's theologian, and was to write thirteen, or fourteen, of the N.T., Epistles ! But his theme, from the beginning, was *Christ, the Son of God* (20), which fact he "*proved* " (22). The people were" *amazed* "(21), not only at the ability and power of the preacher, but at such an one being a preacher at all, who until now had been so bitter a persecutor. But there was *antagonism* as well as *amazement*, as we see in :

(iv) *The Conspiracy against Saul* (23–31). Both pleasure and pain enter into the texture of our life ; but it is never all pain, as it is never all pleasure. Men may kill the preacher, but they cannot kill the Gospel (23). With verse 25 read 2 Cor. xi. 32, 33. The fear of the Jerusalem disciples was quite natural, but Barnabas played the friend, for " a friend in need, is a friend indeed " (26, 27). At this time Saul stayed with Peter for a fortnight (28, Gal. i. 18). Try and imagine how Peter would have talked, and how Saul would have listened, and the places in and around the City they would have visited together ! But Saul was too hot for the hypocrites (29), and so God told him to get away (30, with ch. xxii. 17–21).

Now that a fierce foe had become so faithful a friend, the churches had peace and prosperity (31).

Thought : *THE NOBLEST SERMON IS A CHRISTIAN LIFE.*

THE ACTS ix. 32-43

Title : *AENEAS AND DORCAS*

32 And it came to pass, as Peter passed throughout all quarters, he came down also to the saints which dwelt at Lydda. 33 And there he found a certain man named Æneas, which had kept his bed eight years, and was sick of the palsy. 34 And Peter said unto him, Æneas, Jesus Christ maketh thee whole : arise, and make thy bed. And he arose immediately. 35 And all that dwelt at Lydda and Saron saw him, and turned to the Lord.

36 Now there was at Joppa a certain disciple named Tabitha, which by interpretation is called Dorcas : this woman was full of good works and almsdeeds which she did. 37 And it came to pass in those days, that she was sick, and died : whom when they had washed, they laid her in an upper chamber. 38 And forasmuch as Lydda was nigh to Joppa, and the disciples had heard that Peter was there, they sent unto him two men, desiring him that he would not delay to come to them. 39 Then Peter arose and went with them. When he was come, they brought him unto the upper chamber : and all the widows stood by him weeping, and shewing the coats and garments which Dorcas made, while she was with them. 40 But Peter put them all forth, and kneeled down, and prayed ; and turning him to the body said, Tabitha, arise. And she opened her eyes : and when she saw Peter, she sat up. 41 And he gave her his hand, and lifted her up, and when he had called the saints and widows, presented her alive. 42 And it was known throughout all Joppa ; and many believed in the Lord. 43 And it came to pass, that he tarried many days in Joppa with one Simon a tanner.

EXPOSITION

The next stage in this story is—III. PETER'S PREPARATION FOR THE WIDER WITNESS (ix. 32–x. 48).

1. PETER AT LYDDA (32–35). " *Rest* " is variously regarded and interpreted (31). Peter interpreted it in terms of *work*. He always was a man of energy and enterprise. The leader of the Jerusalem Church made excursions from time to time, and these were fruitful, not only for the places visited, but also for the Church left meanwhile. If your minister is so led, don't complain. Well, a man who had been in bed for eight years gets up, he rises out of weakness into strength, by *power* on God's part, and *faith* on his own. In the absence of either of these factors there is no transition from one state to another. A bodily-absent Christ may be a spiritually-present power. Physical healing may lead to spiritual life, " *all that saw turned to the Lord.*" Has Jesus Christ made thee whole ? (34).

2. PETER AT JOPPA (36–43). There a *man* (33), here a *woman* ; there, healing (34), here, *quickening* ; there " *all* " believed (35), but here, " *many* " (42). God was the power, and Peter the agent in both cases. Both events were miraculous, but widely differ. Dorcas is delivered from death. She was missed and mourned because she had been merciful : the people would not have grieved if Dorcas had not been good ; the wicked are not wailed. Back of this woman's labour was her love. If she came back to earth to-day, imagine her surprise to find everywhere *Dorcas Societies.* From a little seed well sown comes a rich harvest. Surprises await many an unselfish woman. God sees what is obscure, and will reward all that is done for Him. I was going to say that Dorcas deserved to live again, but, upon reflection, was it not a sad thing that she should come back into such a world as this ? Not for her own sake was she brought back, but for the Gospel's, and the Church's. The Bible tells us of nine persons who were raised

from the dead, but not one of them has told us of his or her experience in the other world.

Thought : CHRIST OFFERS US, NOT ONLY LIFE, BUT HEALTH.

THE ACTS x. 1-16

Title : TWO REVELATIONS

1 There was a certain man in Cæsarea called Cornelius, a centurion of the band called the Italian band, 2 A devout man, and one that feared God with all his house, which gave much alms to the people, and prayed to God alway. 3 He saw in a vision evidently about the ninth hour of the day an angel of God coming in to him, and saying unto him, Cornelius. 4 And when he looked on him, he was afraid, and said, What is it, Lord ? And he said unto him, Thy prayers and thine alms are come up for a memorial before God. 5 And now send men to Joppa, and call for one Simon, whose surname is Peter : 6 He lodgeth with one Simon a tanner, whose house is by the sea side : he shall tell thee what thou oughtest to do. 7 And when the angel which spake unto Cornelius was departed, he called two of his household servants, and a devout soldier of them that waited on him continually ; 8 And when he had declared all these things unto them, he sent them to Joppa.

9 On the morrow, as they went on their journey, and drew nigh unto the city, Peter went up upon the housetop to pray about the sixth hour : 10 And he became very hungry, and would have eaten : but while they made ready, he fell into a trance, 11 And saw heaven opened, and a certain vessel descending unto him, as it had been a great sheet knit at the four corners, and let down to the earth : 12 Wherein were all manner of fourfooted beasts of the earth, and wild beasts, and creeping things, and fowls of the air. 13 And there came a voice to him, Rise, Peter ; kill, and eat. 14 But Peter said, Not so, Lord ; for I have never eaten any thing that

is common or unclean. 15 And the voice spake
unto him again the second time, What God hath
cleansed, that call not thou common. 16 This was
done thrice : and the vessel was received up again
into heaven.

EXPOSITION

Peter is still at Joppa (1–23a). This is a chapter of
incalculable importance alike for the Church and the
world. It records nothing less than the formal opening
of the Door of Grace to the Gentiles. Peter, the
apostle of the circumcision, preaches the Gospel to a
Roman official at the latter's house : and this was
his great preparation for the wider witness. Here are
two revelations, and both are preparations. Remember, every revelation is a preparation for something beyond.

(i) *The Revelation to Cornelius the Gentile* (1–8).
This is a fine illustration of the distinction between
religion and Christianity. Christianity is religion,
but all religion is not Christianity. Cornelius was a
religious man, but not yet was he a Christian man.
Note his piety, reverence, influence, liberality,
prayerfulness, receptivity, and obedience. He was
living up to the light he had ; but that was not
enough, it never is. Yet, do not this man's moral
earnestness, simple faith, and genuine humility put
many a Christian to shame ?

Now consider (ii) *The Revelation to Peter the Jew*
(9–16). It would be a great thing if every Christian
in the world prayed for two minutes every day at 12
o'clock (9). Two details here, contribute to weaken
Peter's Jewish prejudices ; first, his residing with a
tanner (ix. 43), involving contact with dead animals ;
second, the wide view he had over the Mediterranean
may have led him to think of the regions beyond.
Well, while they were getting the dinner ready, Peter
fell asleep. That at least kept him from grumbling,
but it did much more : he got a vision, which was
better than the best victuals. Read 11–16 with Levi-

79

ticus **xi**, and you will understand Peter's point of view.

Nowhere in language is so flagrant and fearful a contradiction fixed in three words as in verse 14 : " NOT SO, LORD." Whoever says " *not so*," should never add " *Lord* " ; and whoever truly says " *Lord* " never will say " *not so*." It is not for the servant to dictate to the master. Say to-day whether you will part with the first two words, or with the third.

Thought : GOD HAS SOMETHING TO TEACH THEE TO-DAY. LOOK. LISTEN.

THE ACTS x. 17-33

Title : A MOMENTOUS INTERVIEW

17 Now while Peter doubted in himself what this vision which he had seen should mean, behold, the men which were sent from Cornelius had made enquiry for Simon's house, and stood before the gate. 18 And called, and asked whether Simon, which was surnamed Peter, were lodged there. 19 While Peter thought on the vision, the Spirit said unto him, Behold, three men seek thee. 20 Arise, therefore, and get thee down, and go with them, doubting nothing : for I have sent them. 21 Then Peter went down to the men which were sent unto him from Cornelius ; and said, Behold, I am he whom ye seek : what is the cause wherefore ye are come ? 22 And they said, Cornelius the centurion, a just man, and one that feareth God, and of good report among all the nation of the Jews, was warned from God by an holy angel to send for thee into his house, and to hear words of thee. 23 Then called he them in, and lodged them. And on the morrow Peter went away with them, and certain brethren from Joppa accompanied him.

24 And the morrow after they entered into Cæsarea. And Cornelius waited for them, and had called together his kinsmen and near friends. 25 And as Peter was coming in, Cornelius met

him and fell down at his feet, and worshipped him. 26 But Peter took him up, saying, Stand up ; I myself also am a man. 27 And as he talked with him, he went in, and found many that were come together. 28 And he said unto them, Ye know how that it is an unlawful thing for a man that is a Jew to keep company, or come unto one of another nation ; but God hath shewed me that I should not call any man common or unclean. 29 Therefore came I unto you without gainsaying, as soon as I was sent for : I ask therefore for what intent ye have sent for me ? 30 And Cornelius said, Four days ago I was fasting until this hour ; and at the ninth hour I prayed in my house, and, behold, a man stood before me in bright clothing, 31 And said, Cornelius, thy prayer is heard, and thine alms are had in remembrance in the sight of God. 32 Send therefore to Joppa, and call hither Simon, whose surname is Peter ; he is lodged in the house of one Simon a tanner by the sea side : who, when he cometh, shall speak unto thee. 33 Immediately therefore I sent to thee ; and thou hast well done that thou art come. Now therefore are we all here present before God, to hear all things that are commanded thee of God.

EXPOSITION

History records many interviews between great men : e.g., DIOGENES with ALEXANDER ; LUTHER with CHARLES V. ; MILTON with GALILEO ; GARIBALDI with VICTOR EMANUEL : and LIVINGSTONE with STANLEY ; but none of them was so momentous as that of PETER with CORNELIUS (25). This was one of those hinges upon which, small as they seem, vast interests turn. It was one of those moments when revolutions in the whole state of human society are at the birth ; when that is being unconsciously enacted by the doers which will powerfully affect mankind to the end of time, and beyond it. Christ had given to Peter, " *the keys of the kingdom* " (Matt. xvi. 19), and Peter with them now opens the gates for the entrance of countless millions of Gentile believers. Think about that. *An Israelite shows an Italian the way.*

3. PETER AT CAESAREA (23b–48) : There are wheels within wheels in Divine Providence ; events mesh ; and " *all things work together for good, to them that love God.*" The order here is—revelation, commission, action ; the *vision* is followed by the *voice*, and the voice by the *venture*. Have you seen and heard, and yet have not gone ? Think of those who are waiting for you (24). How much longer are they to wait ?

" A cry as of pain, again and again,
    Is borne o'er the deserts and wide-spreading main ;
    A cry from the lands that in darkness are lying,
    A cry from the hearts that in sorrow are sighing ;
    It comes unto me ; it comes unto thee ;
    Oh, what—oh what shall the answer be ? "

The man who in ch. v. 40 was whipped, is now worshipped (25), but he will have none of it (26). There they are, the Peter party, and the Cornelius party (27). Peter speaks first (28, 29), and then, Cornelius (30–33). The heart of Peter's speech is in the words, " *God hath shewed me* " : and the heart of Cornelius' speech is, " *we are all here present before God, to hear all things that are commanded thee of God.*" This whole thing was a *Godly* affair.

Thought : THERE IS ALWAYS AN OPEN DOOR FOR THE OPEN HEART.

THE ACTS x. 34-48

Title : THE FIRST GENTILE CHURCH

34 Then Peter opened his mouth, and said, Of a truth I perceive that God is no respecter of persons : **35** But in every nation he that feareth him, and worketh righteousness, is accepted with him. **36** The word which God sent unto the children of Israel, preaching peace by Jesus Christ : (he is Lord of all :) **37** That word, I say, ye know, which was published throughout all Judaea, and began from Galilee, after the baptism which John preached ;

38 How God anointed Jesus of Nazareth with the Holy Ghost and with power : who went about doing good, and healing all that were oppressed of the devil ; for God was with him. 39 And we are witnesses of all things which he did both in the land of the Jews, and in Jerusalem ; whom they slew and hanged on a tree : 40 Him God raised up the third day, and shewed him openly ; 41 Not to all the people, but unto witnesses chosen before of God, even to us, who did eat and drink with him after he rose from the dead. 42 And he commanded us to preach unto the people, and to testify that it is he which was ordained of God to be the Judge of quick and dead. 43 To him give all the prophets witness, that through his name whosoever believeth in him shall receive remission of sins.

44 While Peter yet spake these words, the Holy Ghost fell on all them which heard the word. 45 And they of the circumcision which believed were astonished, as many as came with Peter, because that on the Gentiles also was poured out the gift of the Holy Ghost. 46 For they heard them speak with tongues, and magnify God. Then answered Peter, 47 Can any man forbid water, that these should not be baptized, which have received the Holy Ghost as well as we ? 48 And he commanded them to be baptized in the name of the Lord. Then prayed they him to tarry certain days.

EXPOSITION

This portion is of profoundest importance, not only because here is—

1. THE SERMON (34–43), by which the middle wall of partition between Jew and Gentile was broken down, but also because in it we have the fullest specimen which the Church possesses, of a " primitive Gospel," which was widely preached at least a quarter of a century before any of our Gospel Records was committed to writing ; and in this sermon is summarized the leading thought of each of the Four.

Mark's Gospel, which was written at Peter's instigation, is but an expansion of verse 38, in Peter's sermon ; indeed we may say that this, his sixth address, is Mark's Gospel in germ. It is wonderful that within fifteen years of Jesus' death, this staunch Jew has got the length of telling an Italian congregation that " He is Lord of ALL," and " the Judge of quick and dead " (36, 42). Note, it does not say that all *religions* are alike in God's sight, but all *nations* (34, 35).

This is the first trumpet-sound of the Gospel in the heathen world, and its great notes are : the personal Redeemer, the witnessing Church, and the universal invitation. Jesus was more than a Philanthropist, He was a Propitiation ; He was more than a reformer, being a Redeemer. Never let that fact go, for if you do, everything else goes with it that matters. There is no use of any one preaching to any body, at home or abroad, who cannot preach—the Christ Who lived, the Christ Who died, the Christ Who lives again, and the Christ Who can save any one and every one from sin now and for ever.

2. THE RESULT (44-48). This is the first Gentile Church, resting on the same *Rock*, and receiving the same *Seal* as the Jewish Church on the Day of Pentecost. The Gospel is needed by all, is sufficient for all, is accessible to all, and may be received by all. Oh, grand and glorious Gospel ! The gift of the Spirit and speaking with tongues were closely associated in the early Church, but never anywhere does it say that " Tongues " was the evidence of the " Gift." Read this wonderful chapter again and again.

Thought : TRADITION MUST GIVE WAY TO TRUTH.

THE ACTS xi. 1-18

Title : THE FORMIDABILITY OF FACTS

1 And the apostles and brethren that were in Judaea heard that the Gentiles had also received the word of God. 2 And when Peter was come up to

Jerusalem, they that were of the circumcision contended with him, 3 Saying, Thou wentest in to men uncircumcised, and didst eat with them. 4 But Peter rehearsed the matter from the beginning, and expounded it by order unto them, saying,

5 I was in the city of Joppa praying : and in a trance I saw a vision, A certain vessel descend, as it had been a great sheet, let down from heaven by four corners ; and it came even to me : 6 Upon the which when I had fastened mine eyes, I considered, and saw fourfooted beasts of the earth, and wild beasts, and creeping things, and fowls of the air. 7 And I heard a voice saying unto me, Arise, Peter ; slay and eat. 8 But I said, Not so, Lord : for nothing common or unclean hath at any time entered into my mouth. 9 But the voice answered me again from heaven, What God hath cleansed, that call not thou common. 10 And this was done three times : and all were drawn up again into heaven. 11 And, behold, immediately there were three men already come unto the house where I was, sent from Caesarea unto me. 12 And the Spirit bade me go with them, nothing doubting. Moreover these six brethren accompanied me, and we entered into the man's house : 13 And he shewed us how he had seen an angel in his house, which stood and said unto him, Send men to Joppa, and call for Simon, whose surname is Peter ; 14 Who shall tell thee words, whereby thou and all thy house shall be saved. 15 And as I began to speak, the Holy Ghost fell on them, as on us at the beginning. 16 Then remembered I the word of the Lord, how that he said, John indeed baptized with water ; but ye shall be baptized with the Holy Ghost. 17 Forasmuch then as God gave them the like gift as he did unto us, who believed on the Lord Jesus Christ ; what was I, that I could withstand God ?

18 When they heard these things, they held their peace, and glorified God, saying, Then hath God also to the Gentiles granted repentance unto life.

EXPOSITION

We come now to—

IV. The Apostles' Preparation for the Wider Witness (1–18). We have followed Philip's, Saul's, and Peter's ; now the whole body of the Apostles at Jerusalem is to enter into a larger conception of the meaning of Christianity. This is brought about, strangely enough, by way of an *indictment of Peter* for going to Cornelius (1–3). But they had to learn, and so have we, that where there is revelation there must be enlargement, and that what at first is censured, may have at last to be commended. How did Peter meet this charge and censure ? I think I know how he would have met it *before* Pentecost ; but he was another man now. Has the Holy Spirit made any difference in your life ?

Well, in this his seventh address, Peter simply narrates the facts (5–17), declaring that he had done all under Divine direction (5, 9, 12, 15, 16). A fact is a great argument (see iv. 14) ; that is more than abuse ever is, though this is too often resorted to in debate. But, remember, abuse is the refuge of the weak. Peter just tells the story. He does not go behind the facts by trying to explain them ; he is content to affirm them, and to point to the result of his so-called lawless action (x. 28). Peter considers that if an *angel* could stand in the house of a Gentile, an apostle might well do so (13).

Relating the effect upon himself of what had happened, he says, " *then remembered I—*" Here is a lesson on *getting* memory-stores, *keeping* memory-stores, and *using* memory-stores. The first effect, then, was one of *memory* ; the second, was one of *conviction* that this was God's work, and therefore opposed (17). Here we are given to see God's purpose, so striking ; God's plan, so simple ; and God's power, so sufficient. The argument of fact convinced the Apostles (18). How could they " *hold their peace . . . saying* " ? Criticism was silenced when conviction was reached.

Thought : LET US TELL WHAT WE KNOW
         OF GOD'S DOINGS

Title : THE CHURCH IN SYRIAN ANTIOCH

19 Now they which were scattered abroad upon the persecution that arose about Stephen travelled as far as Phenice, and Cyprus, and Antioch, preaching the word to none but unto the Jews only. 20 And some of them were men of Cyprus and Cyrene, which, when they were come to Antioch, spake unto the Grecians, preaching the Lord Jesus. 21 And the hand of the Lord was with them : and a great number believed, and turned unto the Lord. 22 Then tidings of these things came unto the ears of the church which was in Jerusalem : and they sent forth Barnabas, that he should go as far as Antioch. 23 Who, when he came, and had seen the grace of God, was glad, and exhorted them all, that with purpose of heart they would cleave unto the Lord. 24 For he was a good man, and full of the Holy Ghost and of faith : and much people were added unto the Lord. 25 Then departed Barnabas to Tarsus, for to seek Saul : 26 And when he had found him, he brought him unto Antioch. And it came to pass, that a whole year they assembled themselves with the church, and taught much people. And the disciples were called Christians first in Antioch.

27 And in these days came prophets from Jerusalem unto Antioch. 28 And there stood up one of them named Agabus, and signified by the Spirit that there should be great dearth throughout all the world : which came to pass in the days of Claudius Caesar. 29 Then the disciples, every man according to his ability, determined to send relief unto the brethren which dwelt in Judaea : 30 Which also they did, and sent it to the elders by the hands of Barnabas and Saul.

EXPOSITION

There remains one more stage in this TRANSITION PERIOD (viii. 5 to xii. 25), namely :—

V. THE CHURCH'S PREPARATION FOR THE WIDER WITNESS (xi. 19–xii. 25). Here, let us observe three things.

1. THE PROGRESS OF THE CHURCH AT ANTIOCH

(19–30). Verse 19 connects directly with viii. 1–4, and what follows (19–21) is independent of all that has happened between these passages, namely, viii. 5 to xi. 18. The establishment of a Christian Church in Antioch in Syria was a momentous event. The city is said to have had a population of 500,000. It was one of the three largest cities in the Roman Empire, and was famed for its commerce, art, literature, and infamous for its vice and frivolity. Just the place for a Christian Church. The founding of it was in three stages, marked by the arrival of *travelling preachers* (19–21), of *Barnabas* (22–24), and of *Saul* (25, 26). Barnabas seems to have had an unusual power of doing the right thing at the right time (cf. iv. 36 ; ix. 27 ; xi. 23, 24). This is something we should all covet and cultivate. The advice of Barnabas to those people we well may take to ourselves. " *With purpose of heart to cleave unto the Lord* " (23). We need tenacity in the hour of temptation. Mark the new name, " *Christians* " (26) ; given to the disciples by the heathen at Antioch in jest or mockery. But what a superb jest, containing, as the word does, *Hebrew thought*, equivalent of *Messiah* ; *Greek language* in the substantive *Christ* ; and a *Latin element* in " ians," and in this way reflecting the universality of the Gospel. Compare Luke xxiii. 38. Life is energetic, and love is sacrificial, and so a collection is taken up (27–30). Until now we have read of Apostles and Deacons ; here are also Prophets (27), and Elders (30). The two great parts of the Church are drawing together, and Gentile Christians are helping Christian Jews (29). Soon the ideas *Gentile* and *Jew* were to die, and only *Christian*, be left.

Thought : THE WAY TO BE GOOD IS TO BE FILLED WITH THE SPIRIT (24).

THE ACTS xii. 1-12

Title : PETER IN PRISON

1 Now about that time Herod the king stretched forth his hands to vex certain of the church. 2 And

he killed James the brother of John with the sword. 3 And because he saw it pleased the Jews, he proceeded further to take Peter also. (Then were the days of unleavened bread.) 4 And when he had apprehended him, he put him in prison, and delivered him to four quaternions of soldiers to keep him ; intending after Easter to bring him forth to the people. 5 Peter therefore was kept in prison : but prayer was made without ceasing of the church unto God for him.

6 And when Herod would have brought him forth, the same night Peter was sleeping between two soldiers, bound with two chains : and the keepers before the door kept the prison. 7 And, behold, the angel of the Lord came upon him, and a light shined in the prison : and he smote Peter on the side, and raised him up, saying, Arise up quickly. And his chains fell off from his hands. 8 And the angel said unto him, Gird thyself, and bind on thy sandals. And so he did. And he saith unto him, Cast thy garment about thee, and follow me. 9 And he went out, and followed him ; and wist not that it was true which was done by the angel ; but thought he saw a vision. 10 When they were past the first and the second ward, they came unto the iron gate that leadeth unto the city ; which opened to them of his own accord : and they went out, and passed on through one street : and forthwith the angel departed from him.

11 And when Peter was come to himself, he said Now I know of a surety, that the Lord hath sent his angel, and hath delivered me out of the hand of Herod, and from all the expectation of the people of the Jews. 12 And when he had considered the thing, he came to the house of Mary the mother of John, whose surname was Mark ; where many were gathered together praying.

EXPOSITION

Now follows 2. THE PERSECUTION OF THE CHURCH AT JERUSALEM (1–23). Here are the execution of one murder, and the contemplation of another. What for ? To please the Jews (3). This is a chapter of

sharp contrasts. Over against the love of the Gentiles
(xi. 29, 30) is the hate of the Jews (3) ; over against
the death of one apostle is the deliverance of another ;
over against a king's power is a subject's weakness ;
over against armed security is angelic salvation ;
over against cruel purpose (4) is Divine protection.
Before bidding farewell to James, brother of John,
and one of the Three, review his history (John i. 41 ;
Matt. iv. 21 ; Matt. x. 2 ; Mark v. 37 ; Matt. xvii. 1 ;
Luke ix. 54 ; Mark x. 35 ; xiii. 3 ; xiv. 33 ; Acts i. 13 ;
ii. 4 ; I Cor. xv. 7 ; Acts xii. 2). The second martyr
goes. Blessed are the dead who die, not only " *in* "
but *for* the Lord.

Herod intended to make a great spectacle of
Peter's death, after the Passover Feast (4), but he
reckoned without God. Observe, however, what
precautions he took to keep his victim secure (4, 6).
" BUT PRAYER " (5). Yes, that alters the whole
situation. Does your case seem hopeless ? " *But
prayer.*" Are the odds all against you ? " *But
prayer.*" And observe that this prayer was (a)
without ceasing ; (b) *of the church* ; (c) *unto God* ;
(d) *for him* (5) ; that is, it was persistent, united,
worshipful and definite. In reply God brought
deliverance ; but He waited until the last night (6),
and the last moment (18), between three and six
o'clock in the morning. He never is before His
time, and He never is behind.

Verses 6–10 are very graphic. Look ! Four
soldiers (4), two chains, keepers (6), an iron gate, and
two wards (10) ! And there is the man off to see
some friends of his (12) ! Heaven has played a
trick on Herod : an angel has made him look
foolish. But though miraculously delivered, Peter
must exercise common sense ; he must think
quickly and act promptly, or it will be " as you
were " (11, 12).

Thought : THINK OF THE LEISURELINESS OF
       GOD (8).

Title : THE ROUT OF WRONG

13 And as Peter knocked at the door of the gate, a damsel came to hearken, named Rhoda. 14 And when she knew Peter's voice, she opened not the gate for gladness, but ran in, and told how Peter stood before the gate. 15 And they said unto her, Thou art mad. But she constantly affirmed that it was even so. Then said they, It is his angel. 16 But Peter continued knocking : and when they had opened the door, and saw him, they were astonished. 17 But he, beckoning unto them with the hand to hold their peace, declared unto them how the Lord had brought him out of the prison. And he said, Go shew these things unto James, and to the brethren. And he departed and went into another place. 18 Now as soon as it was day, there was no small stir among the soldiers, what was become of Peter. 19 And when Herod had sought for him, and found him not, he examined the keepers, and commanded that they should be put to death. And he went down from Judaea to Caesarea, and there abode.

20 And Herod was highly displeased with them of Tyre and Sidon : but they came with one accord to him, and, having made Blastus the king's chamberlain their friend, desired peace ; because their country was nourished by the king's country. 21 And upon a set day, Herod, arrayed in royal apparel, sat upon his throne, and made an oration unto them. 22 And the people gave a shout, saying, It is the voice of a god and not of a man. 23 And immediately the angel of the Lord smote him, because he gave not God the glory : and he was eaten of worms, and gave up the ghost.

24 But the word of God grew and multiplied.

25 And Barnabas and Saul returned from Jerusalem, when they had fulfilled their ministry, and took with them John, whose surname was Mark.

EXPOSITION

Persecution of the Church at Jerusalem (1–23). The delivered Peter, " *having grasped the situation* " (12) resolved to go to the home of Mary, the mother of John Mark. No doubt Peter had often stayed there ; and, no doubt, that hospitable dwelling was the birthplace of Mark's Gospel. Now, remember, these people were praying for Peter's deliverance (12), yet when he turned up at the house, they did not believe that it was he, and called the maid " *raving mad* " for saying he was there (15) ; and as she " *kept confidently asserting* " the fact, they then concluded that it was " *his angel* " ; and when the door was opened, Peter having been kept there knocking, and they beheld him, " *they were amazed.*"

What a way to pray ! It may be well to remind ourselves that prayer is not an end in itself, but a means to an end, so that when the means is made the end, the end is never reached. If God answered your prayers, would *you* be astonished ? Let us frankly acknowledge that the answers we get to our prayers are not of our merit, but of His mercy. God does better for us than we deserve.

But, what has become of Peter ? (18). Peter was a problem : Christians often are to the world. And there is another, a moral problem, here. These " keepers " were not responsible for either Peter's imprisonment, or his escape ; yet, they were " put to death " (19). That is part of an age-long and world-wide problem, the sufferings of the innocent, and we must just leave it.

Now follows a solemn lesson on *Presumption and Punishment* (20–23). Pride goes too far when it reaches to the throne of God (22). 'Tis then that He makes men know that truth is not always on the scaffold. The same angel who saves believers (7) smites blasphemers (23). Rebellion and retribution are never far apart. But, in spite of persecution the Church prospers. Mark this progress so far : ii. 41 ; iv. 4, 32 ; v. 14 ; vi. 7 ; viii. 4, 25 ; ix. 31, 32 ; xi. 24.

Thought : RIGHT IS RESISTLESS.

Title : *THE BEGINNING OF WORLD
EVANGELIZATION*

1 Now there were in the church that was at
Antioch certain prophets and teachers ; as Barnabas,
and Simeon that was called Niger, and Lucius of
Cyrene, and Manaen, which had been brought up
with Herod the tetrarch, and Saul. 2 As they
ministered to the Lord, and fasted, the Holy Ghost
said, Separate me Barnabas and Saul for the work
whereunto I have called them. 3 And when they
had fasted and prayed, and laid their hands on them,
they sent them away.

4 So they, being sent forth by the Holy Ghost,
departed unto Seleucia : and from thence they sailed
to Cyprus. 5 And when they were at Salamis, they
preached the word of God in the synagogues of the
Jews : and they had also John to their minister.
6 And when they had gone through the isle unto
Paphos, they found a certain sorcerer, a false prophet
a Jew, whose name was Bar-jesus : 7 Which was
with the deputy of the country, Sergius Paulus, a
prudent man ; who called for Barnabas and Saul, and
desired to hear the word of God. 8 But Elymas the
sorcerer (for so is his name by interpretation) with-
stood them, seeking to turn away the deputy from
the faith. 9 Then Saul, (who also is called Paul,)
filled with the Holy Ghost, set his eyes on him,
10 And said, O full of all subtilty and all mischief,
thou child of the devil, thou enemy of all righteousness, wilt thou not cease to pervert the right ways of
the Lord ? 11 And now, behold, the hand of the Lord
is upon thee, and thou shalt be blind, not seeing the
sun for a season. And immediately there fell on him
a mist and a darkness ; and he went about seeking
some to lead him by the hand. 12 Then the deputy,
when he saw what was done, believed, being astonished at the doctrine of the Lord.

EXPOSITION

We enter now upon the third and last main division
of this Book, (C) THE GENTILE PERIOD OF THE

CHURCH'S WITNESS (chs. 13 to 28). (A) was THE JEWISH PERIOD; and (B) was THE TRANSITION PERIOD. The Church which was first FOUNDED, and then BROADENED, is now to be EXTENDED. Ch. xii. 23, was in A.D. 44; xii. 24, 25, covers A.D. 45–48; and ch. xiii, dates from A.D. 48, eighteen years after Christ's Ascension.

This third division of " *Acts* " is in two main parts: Paul's Tireless Activities, and his Fruitful Captivities. Detailed analysis we shall mark as we go.

I. PAUL'S TIRELESS ACTIVITIES (xiii. 1 to xxi. 14). A.D. 44–58.

1. THE FIRST MISSIONARY JOURNEY (xiii. 1 to **xv**. 35) A.D. 45–51. Keep a map of Paul's journeys before you, and trace carefully the route. But there is first of all (i) *The Call and Consecration* (1–3). Barnabas and Saul were selected, separated, and sent forth by the Church at Antioch, not Jerusalem, observe. But the thing of sovereign importance is that *God had called them* (2). Apart from this fact the Church's action would have had no significance or value. *Christian calling is the call of Christ.* Have you heard it? Have you obeyed?

And now, (ii) *The Start* (4–12). Every one whom God chooses is sent forth by the Spirit (4); there is no use starting unless you are. The route taken was by SELEUCIA to SALAMIS, through CYPRUS to PAPHOS. Mark was with them (5). Passing through the isle may have occupied several weeks (6). With verses 6–12, compare viii. 9–24. BAR-JESUS represents Sorcery; SERGIUS PAULUS represents Rationalism; and PAUL represents Christianity. The last judged the first and saved the second. SAUL was Paul's Græco-Roman name, and PAUL was Saul's Hebrew name. From now (9) he is called PAUL, and dominates the situation. No good work is unopposed (8). The triumphs of the Gospel are many and great (12).

Thought: *YOU DO NOT NEED TO GO ABROAD TO BECOME A MISSIONARY.*

Title : HISTORY READ FROM HEAVEN

13 Now when Paul and his company loosed from Paphos, they came to Perga in Pamphylia : and John departing from them returned to Jerusalem. 14 But when they departed from Perga, they came to Antioch in Pisidia, and went into the synagogue on the Sabbath day, and sat down. 15 And after the reading of the law and the prophets the rulers of the synagogue sent unto them, saying, Ye men and brethren, if ye have any word of exhortation for the people, say on. 16 Then Paul stood up, and beckoning with his hand said,

Men of Israel, and ye that fear God, give audience. 17 The God of this people of Israel chose our fathers, and exalted the people when they dwelt as strangers in the land of Egypt, and with an high arm brought he them out of it. 18 And about the time of forty years suffered he their manners in the wilderness. 19 And when he had destroyed seven nations in the land of Chanaan, he divided their land to them by lot. 20 And after that he gave unto them judges about the space of four hundred and fifty years, until Samuel the prophet. 21 And afterward they desired a king : and God gave unto them Saul the son of Cis, a man of the tribe of Benjamin, by the space of forty years. 22 And when he had removed him, he raised up unto them David to be their king ; to whom also he gave testimony, and said, I have found David the son of Jesse, a man after mine own heart, which shall fulfil all my will. 23 Of this man's seed hath God according to his promise raised unto Israel a Saviour Jesus : 24 When John had first preached before his coming the baptism of repentance to all the people of Israel. 25 And as John fulfilled his course, he said, Whom think ye that I am ? I am not he. But, behold, there cometh one after me, whose shoes of his feet I am not worthy to loose.

EXPOSITION

Sketch an outline map of the world of Paul's Journeys, by placing some tracing paper over any good map, using one piece of tracing paper for each Missionary Journey, in order to have the precise route in each case brought clearly before you. Fill in on your blank map the places named in the preceding portion, and now add, PERGA and ANTIOCH in Pisidia. From Paphos to Perga was over one hundred and fifty miles by sea. At Perga, Mark left the other two (13). Why ? Was it fear ? jealousy ? cowardice ? or change of plan ? At any rate, we know the result : xv. 36-40. Mark lost the greatest chance of his life, but eventually he ' made good ' : see 2 Tim. iv. 11, and the Second Gospel. Never reconcile yourself to contentment with the second best. PERGA to ANTIOCH, one hundred miles as the crow flies. Remember they were not motoring, but walking, and Paul was ill. ANTIOCH, an important military and administrative centre. There were strangers at the Jewish Church that next Sabbath (14), and they were given a chance to speak (15). Paul took it, and here we have his first *recorded* sermon (cf. v. 12), verses 16-41. It is in three main parts ; 16-25 : 26-37 : and 38-41.

1. A BRIEF SUMMARY OF ISRAEL'S HISTORY IN ITS DIVINE ASPECT (16-25). This reaches from ABRAM to JOHN THE BAPTIST, being more comprehensive, and much more condensed than Stephen's outline (ch. vii). All is leading up to JESUS and the Good News in the next part of the message. The apostle traces the providential course of Israel's history, and shows that it moved steadily to a consummation which was reached in the Incarnation and its purposes and consequences. Genesis xii. to Exodus xii. is in verse 17 ; Exodus xii to the end of Deuteronomy is in verse 18 ; the Book of Joshua is in verse 19 ; the Book of Judges, Ruth and 1 Samuel 1-7 are in verse 20 ; I Samuel viii. to I Kings ii. is in verses 21, 22 ; and in the words " *of this man's seed*," in verse 23, history is summarized from 1 Kings ii. to the birth of Jesus. Through these ages one increasing purpose ran. History is His story.

Thought : WE ARE ALL IN THE PLAN OF THE AGES.

Title : THE CHRISTIAN GOSPEL

26 Men and brethren, children of the stock of Abraham, and whosoever among you feareth God, to you is the word of this salvation sent. 27 For they that dwell at Jerusalem, and their rulers, because they knew him not, nor yet the voices of the prophets which are read every Sabbath day, they have fulfilled them in condemning him. 28 And though they found no cause of death in him, yet desired they Pilate that he should be slain. 29 And when they had fulfilled all that was written of him, they took him down from the tree, and laid him in a sepulchre. 30 But God raised him from the dead : 31 And he was seen many days of them which came up with him from Galilee to Jerusalem, who are his witnesses unto the people. 32 And we declare unto you glad tidings, how that the promise which was made unto the fathers, 33 God hath fulfilled the same unto us their children, in that he hath raised up Jesus again ; as it is also written in the second psalm, Thou art my Son, this day have I begotten thee. 34 And as concerning that he raised him up from the dead, now no more to return to corruption, he said on this wise, I will give you the sure mercies of David. 35 Wherefore he saith also in another psalm, Thou shalt not suffer thine Holy One to see corruption. 36 For David, after he had served his own generation by the will of God fell on sleep, and was laid unto his fathers and saw corruption : 37 But he, whom God raised again, saw no corruption. 38 Be it known unto you therefore, men and brethren, that through this man is preached unto you the forgiveness of sins : 39 And by him all that believe are justified from all things from which ye could not be justified by the law of Moses. 40 Beware therefore, lest that come upon you, which is spoken of in the prophets ; 41 Behold, ye despisers, and wonder, and perish : for I work a work in your days, a work which ye shall in no wise believe, though a man declare it unto you.

EXPOSITION

The three parts of Paul's Sermon are marked by address : " *Men of Israel, and ye that fear God, give audience* " (16) ; " *Men and brethren,*" (26) ; and " *Be it known unto you therefore, men and brethren* " (38). In the second part of the sermon :

2. THE FACT OF CHRIST'S COMING IS EXPLAINED AND CONFIRMED (26–37). If in the previous part we have a summary of Israel's history, in preparation for Christ, in this part, we have a summary of the Gospel, the great notes of which are the *Death*, and *Resurrection* of JESUS, providing and proclaiming *salvation*. This is still more condensed in 1 Cor. xv. 3, 4. These were also the dominating notes of Peter's Pentecostal Sermon ; and his and Paul's Epistles are but amplifications and interpretations of " *the Word of this salvation* " (26).

The characteristics of this sermon are its comprehensiveness, brevity, directness, insight, conviction, earnestness, cogency, and power ; and the best sermons will always possess these qualities. Let us learn from Paul how to preach.

Now, we'll mark a few details. We may read the Bible without understanding it (27).

Man's sin may fulfil God's purpose, but its guilt is in no wise diminished (27).

We have not always a sufficient reason for what we do (28).

" *They laid Him in a sepulchre, but God raised Him from the dead.*" God will not do what we can, and we cannot do what God will. Jesus was put into the grave by a human act, but He came out of it by a Divine act. (29, 30).

The resurrection was the fulfilment of promise (32, 33).

" *Begotten* " in Psalm ii. 7, does not refer to Christ's *birth*, but to His resurrection.

Mark the three O.T. quotations (33-35). Psalm xvi. 10 cannot refer to David or to any one but Jesus (35, 37).

" *David served his own generation by the will of*

God ; then fell on sleep " (36). This calls our attention to the sacrament, the sphere, and the standard of Christian service.

This wonderful Sermon is brought to an end by : 3. AN OFFER AND A WARNING (38–41). Here His humanity and Divinity are seen in indissoluble unity. Only God can forgive sins ; Jesus forgave sins ; therefore Jesus is God (38). Here, also, we see the superiority of the Gospel over the Law. The former does what the latter could not (39). And finally, we are reminded that privilege always entails responsibility. Offer makes possible refusal. *Justification and forgiveness* are only by " *this man.*"

Thought : CHRIST'S RESURRECTION COM-
        PLETES OUR REDEMPTION.

THE ACTS xiii. 42-52

Title : FOR AND AGAINST

42 And when the Jews were gone out of the synagogue, the Gentiles besought that these words might be preached to them the next sabbath. **43** Now when the congregation was broken up, many of the Jews and religious proselytes followed Paul and Barnabas : who, speaking to them, persuaded them to continue in the grace of God.

44 And the next sabbath day came almost the whole city together to hear the word of God. **45** But when the Jews saw the multitudes, they were filled with envy, and spake against those things which were spoken by Paul, contradicting and blaspheming. **46** Then Paul and Barnabas waxed bold, and said, It was necessary that the word of God should first have been spoken to you : but seeing ye put it from you, and judge yourselves unworthy of everlasting life, lo, we turn to the Gentiles. **47** For so hath the Lord commanded us, saying, I have set thee to be a light of the Gentiles, that thou shouldest be for salvation unto the ends of the earth.

48 And when the Gentiles heard this, they were glad, and glorified the word of the Lord : and as many as were ordained to eternal life believed. 49 And the word of the Lord was published throughout all the region. 50 But the Jews stirred up the devout and honourable women, and the chief men of the city, and raised persecution against Paul and Barnabas, and expelled them out of their coasts. 51 But they shook off the dust of their feet against them, and came unto Iconium. 52 And the disciples were filled with joy, and with the Holy Ghost.

EXPOSITION

The Missionary Circuit in Asia Minor is recorded in xiii. 4 to xiv. 28. The *Outward Journey* in xiii. 4 to xiv. 20 : and the *Inward Journey* in xiv. 21-28. Follow, and memorize, the names of the places visited on the outward journey. Here are the initials : A.S.S.P.P.A.I.L.D.

This passage is full of power, in the way alike of encouragement and warning. We are shown what constitutes success in Christian service. The worker will awaken in the minds of others, interest and inquiry relative to the Gospel (42-44) ; he will follow this up by encouragement (43) ; if one door is closed, he will enter any that is open (46) ; he will learn that God's work is sometimes accomplished by means of opposition (46-48) ; he will be prepared for some disappointments (45-50) ; and he will find that holy joy is possible, opposition not withstanding (52).

The Gospel always has been revealing, and it ever has had opposite effects upon those who have heard it. The same sun which hardens brick, melts butter. The Gospel is to some a savour of life, and to others, of death. All these people had the same opportunity ; they heard the same message, from the same preacher, but some of them believed and others blasphemed (45). When opportunity passes from one, it passes to another (46). A man's relation to Jesus Christ is his verdict on himself (46).

100

The Gospel never was intended for the Jews only (47). Why should it be ? Light was created before the sun. Persecution is the last resort of the defeated. Abuse is no substitute for argument. Women can powerfully help or hinder the course of any movement in the world (50). Let the women rise up as an army against intemperance and impurity, and these will quit the field. Joy in Christ is not in spite of sorrow, but often is promoted by it. " The fruit of the Spirit is joy " (52).

*Thought : LIVE IN CHRIST, NOT IN CIRCUM-
STANCES.*

THE ACTS xiv. 1-18

Title : PAUL AMONG PAGANS

1 And it came to pass in Iconium, that they went both together into the synagogue of the Jews, and so spake, that a great multitude both of the Jews and also of the Greeks believed. 2 But the unbelieving Jews stirred up the Gentiles, and made their minds evil affected against the brethren. 3 Long time therefore abode they speaking boldly in the Lord, which gave testimony unto the word of his grace, and granted signs and wonders to be done by their hands. 4 But the multitude of the city was divided : and part held with the Jews, and part with the apostles. 5 And when there was an assault made both of the Gentiles, and also of the Jews with their rulers, to use them despitefully, and to stone them, 6 They were aware of it and fled unto Lystra and Derbe, cities of Lycaonia, and unto the region that lieth round about : 7 And there they preached the gospel.

8 And there sat a certain man at Lystra, impotent in his feet, being a cripple from his mother's womb, who had never walked : 9 The same heard Paul speak : who steadfastly beholding him, and perceiving that he had faith to be healed, 10 Said with a loud voice, Stand upright on thy feet. And he leaped

and walked. 11 And when the people saw what Paul had done, they lifted up their voices saying in the speech of Lycaonia, The gods are come down to us in the likeness of men. 12 And they called Barnabas, Jupiter; and Paul, Mercurius, because he was the chief speaker. 13 Then the priest of Jupiter, which was before their city, brought oxen and garlands unto the gates, and would have done sacrifice with the people. 14 Which when the apostles, Barnabas and Paul heard of, they rent their clothes, and ran in among the people, crying out, 15 And saying, Sirs, why do ye these things? We also are men of like passions with you, and preach unto you that ye should turn from these vanities unto the living God, which made heaven, and earth, and the sea, and all things that are therein: 16 Who in times past suffered all nations to walk in their own ways. 17 Nevertheless he left not himself without witness, in that he did good, and gave us rain from heaven, and fruitful seasons, filling our hearts with food and gladness. 18 And with these sayings scarce restrained they the people, that they had not done sacrifice unto them.

EXPOSITION

AT ICONIUM (1-6). The Divine programme in this dispensation is, not the *conversion*, but the *evangelization* of the world. The bearers of the News are not to remain in any one place until all who are there believe, but are to deliver the message and pass on (xiii. 51; xiv. 6). The word *News* unwittingly testifies to the universality of the Gospel, being the initial letters of North, East, West, South.

Four groups are found in our paragraph : 1. believing Jews and Gentiles (1); 2. unbelieving Jews and Gentiles (2); 3. two parties in the city (3); and 4. Jews, Gentiles, and rulers organized for assault (4).

Paul and Barnabas, now for the first time called " *apostles* " (4), held on until death was in sight, and then they did not flee because they were afraid, but because there was yet much for them to do in the world (6). Christians should show caution and care as well as courage. " *And so spake* " (1) should be considered by all preachers. Think of the matter, manner, secret, and effects of their speech.

AT LYSTRA (6-20). Consider, the crippled man, the pagan populace, and the Apostles. Luke would make it clear that this man was beyond human aid (8) ; but he had faith, and the Apostles had faith in his faith, and so the impossible was done (8-10). No unrepentant sinner has ever walked with God (Amos iii. 3), and the journey cannot be commenced until *faith* meets *power*. At Lystra the Apostles were working for the first time among pure pagans. Mark their excitement and superstition (11-13). The circumstances were a test of the Apostles' loyalty to Christ : observe how they came out of the test (14, 18).

Carefully consider Paul's address to these people (15-17), and mark its contrast to those which have preceded ; and account for this by the audience and object. Here, God is Creator (15), Controller of nations (16), and Giver of all good (17).

Thought : FIGHT, NOT TO LOSE OR TO DRAW, BUT TO WIN.

THE ACTS xiv. 19-28

Title : HOMEWARD BOUND

19 And there came thither certain Jews from Antioch and Iconium, who persuaded the people, and, having stoned Paul, drew him out of the city, supposing he had been dead. 20 Howbeit, as the disciples stood round about him, he rose up and came into the city : and the next day he departed with Barnabas to Derbe. 21 And when they had preached the gospel to that city, and had taught many, they returned again to Lystra, and to Iconium, and Antioch, 22 Confirming the souls of the disciples, and exhorting them to continue in the faith, and that we must through much tribulation enter into the kingdom of God. 23 And when they had ordained them elders in every church, and had prayed with

fasting, they commended them to the Lord, on whom they believed. 24 And after they had passed throughout Pisidia, they came to Pamphylia. 25 And when they had preached the word in Perga, they went down into Attalia : 26 And thence sailed to Antioch, from whence they had been recommended to the grace of God for the work which they fulfilled. 27 And when they were come, and had gathered the church together, they rehearsed all that God had done with them, and how he had opened the door of faith unto the Gentiles. 28 And there they abode long time with the disciples.

EXPOSITION

The Apostles are at LYSTRA still. No good work goes unchallenged : evil men are always active ; and religious appreciation which has its source in the human heart, may easily turn to religious persecution : all that is in verse 19. In spiritual matters, where there is not faith there will be fickleness. Pity the man who trusts the crowd. If it is *Hosanna* to-day, it may be *Crucify* to-morrow. Stoning was a terrible ordeal : what Paul *saw* in ch. vii. 58 ; he *felt* here (2 Cor. xi. 25). Why was not Barnabas stoned ? Miraculously raised, Paul left the town, but not before he had secured his dearest, and perhaps, most useful convert, Timothy (xvi. 1).

AT DERBE (20, 21). A brief record of a great work. The preaching of the Gospel should always have for its aim and end the making of disciples (21, margin).

And now begins *The Inward Journey* (21). What a noble word is this—" *they returned again to Lystra* " ; back to the storm and the stones. That is what missionaries have been doing from the beginning ; they are doing it to-day in China.

The places re-visited are—L.I.A.P.A.A. But this was not just a retracing of steps. Outward bound theirs was a work of *converting ;* homeward bound, it is a work of *confirming* (22). The converts were encouraged, elders were ordained, and all were instructed that the path to triumph was one of tribulation (22, 23) ; and having prayed with and for them, the Apostles left for home, preaching the Word as occasion offered (23–25).

And now they are *Back at the Base* (26–28). Let Greek students compare " *commended* " in 23 and 26. The missionaries return and report. What they had gone forth to do, they had " *fulfilled* " (26). Shall we be able to say that at the end of our life ? (2 Tim. iv. 7). Yet it was GOD Who did what they had done (27). When He opens a door who can shut it ? (27. Rev. iii. 8).

Thought : STAND UP TO THE STONES (19, 21).

THE ACTS xv. 1-3

Title : A PROBLEM ARISES

1 And certain men which came down from Judæa taught the brethren, and said, Except ye be circumcised after the manner of Moses ye cannot be saved. 2 When therefore Paul and Barnabas had no small dissension and disputation with them, they determined that Paul and Barnabas, and certain other of them, should go up to Jerusalem unto the apostles and elders about this question. 3 And being brought on their way by the church, they passed through Phenice and Samaria, declaring the conversion of the Gentiles : and they caused great joy unto all the brethren.

EXPOSITION.

This chapter is of incalculable importance in Church history, recording, as it does, the proceedings of the *First Great Christian Council.* Some idea of its importance may be gathered from the fact that

Peter, and Paul, and James the Lord's brother attended it, the last of these presiding. Here also, we have the earliest example of a Christian letter, and it contains the *Charter of Gentile Christian Liberty*. Read verses 1–35 carefully, together with Galatians ii. 1–10. The majority of commentators consider that these passages are complementary narratives, describing different aspects of the same event. What, then, is it all about?

For background we should read again chs. viii, x, xi, xiii, 46–48, and Gal. i. During the early years of the Christian Church its members were converted Jews only, and not until the dispersion from Jerusalem which followed on the martyrdom of Stephen, was the Gospel preached to the Gentiles. We have seen that in chs. viii to xii, Philip, Saul, Peter, the Apostles, and the whole Church were prepared for a wider witness, that is, for a mission to Gentiles. Following that came Paul's first missionary journey (xiii and xiv), from which, at this time, he has returned. But for all this, the event of ch. xv, would never have occurred. The problem arose out of the conversion of Gentiles. A great blessing precipitated a grave crisis, and often since then problems for the Church have been occasioned by her successes.

The point at issue here is whether or not Christian Gentiles should be circumcised. "*Certain men from Judea*" had gone to Antioch in Syria and were teaching that circumcision was essential for salvation (1); that the Mosaic Law, ceremonial as well as moral, must be obeyed by the Gentiles if they would attach themselves to the Church. This, of course, raised a matter of vital importance. Was Christianity to be but a Christianised Judaism? Could the Christian Church have existence only within the Jewish Church? These implications of the present demand were firmly opposed by Paul and Barnabas, and *not a little commotion and discussion* ensued (2a), and as there seemed no prospect of the parties coming to an understanding, it was agreed that the matter

106

be submitted to the authorities in Jerusalem (26), and so the company went south, at the expense of the Church.

On the way these messengers travelled by Tyre, Sidon, and Samaria, and everywhere caused great joy by "*declaring the conversion of the Gentiles.*" No doubt they chose this theme because of its bearing on the matter about which they were going to Jerusalem.

Thought : THE CHURCH HAS HER DIFFICULTIES.

ACTS xv. 4-12

Title : THE JERUSALEM CONFERENCE

4 And when they were come to Jerusalem, they were received of the church, and of the apostles and elders, and they declared all things that God had done with them. **5** But there rose up certain of the sect of the Pharisees which believed, saying, That it was needful to circumcise them, and to command them to keep the law of Moses.

6 And the apostles and elders came together for to consider of this matter. **7** And when there had been much disputing, Peter rose up, and said unto them,

Men and brethren, ye know how that a good while ago God made choice among us, that the Gentiles by my mouth should hear the word of the gospel, and believe. **8** And God, which knoweth the hearts, bare them witness, giving them the Holy Ghost, even as he did unto us ; **9** And put no difference between us and them, purifying their hearts by faith. **10** Now therefore why tempt ye God, to put a yoke upon the neck of the disciples, which neither our fathers nor we were able to bear ? **11** But we believe that through the grace of the Lord Jesus Christ we shall be saved, even as they.

12 Then all the multitude kept silence, and gave

audience to Barnabas and Paul, declaring what miracles and wonders God had wrought among the Gentiles by them.

EXPOSITION

Well, the party arrive at Jerusalem and are formally received by the Church, the apostles, and the elders there, and without delay they "*rehearsed all things that God had done with them.*" That must have been a profoundly interesting report, the substance of which we have in chs. xiii, xiv. We can imagine how astonished and thrilled the listeners would be as Paul and Barnabas related their experiences, and told of the founding of churches throughout Galatia, in which were both Jews and Gentiles who confessed the name of Christ.

"*But*" (5). Almost certainly, where good work is being done, there will be somebody who has an objection to raise, a criticism to offer, or some word of discouragement to speak. These people are Christians, but they are great in "buts." So here, "*certain of the Pharisees who believed*" expressed themselves to the effect that this good work needed safeguarding; these Gentile converts must toe the line of the Law (5). These men were so rooted in tradition that they had not felt the thrill; they were so loyal to the Law as to imagine that there was an element of danger in the Gospel. At any rate, their view expressed raised the whole question at Jerusalem which had been discussed at Antioch.

No doubt an interval of some days is to be allowed between verses 5 and 6, and then a great assembly met to consider this matter. Observe the constitution of this assembly. There were present Paul and Barnabas and "*certain other*" from Antioch (2); there were these objecting "*Pharisees who believed*" (5), "*the apostles and elders*" (6), and a "*multitude*" of the Jerusalem Church members (12).

And now, here as at Antioch, there was much

" *discussion* " (7, 2), in which, it appears, the members of the Church joined, for at a later moment they " *kept silence* " (12), a reference which would be pointless if they had been silent all the time.

After this general discussion *Peter* rose to address the assembly (7). That was an interesting and critical moment. How all eyes would be turned upon him who was recognised as the apostle of the circumcision (Gal. ii. 7, 8), and how specially anxious Paul would be, wondering what line Peter would take.

What line he did take is told in verses 7–11, which read again carefully. Of course, this is not the full address, but Luke's notes, but they are adequate for the purpose of the record. The speech is in two parts. In the first (7–9) is *a statement of facts*. The speaker takes his stand on *an event*, the conversion, through his instrumentality, of Cornelius and other Gentiles (ch. x), and on *their knowledge of it* (7 ; ch. xi). He reminds them that these Gentiles had received the great evidence of conversion, the Holy Spirit (8), and that in this experience they were in no respect inferior to Jewish believers ; they had exercised saving faith, and their hearts had been cleansed (9). These were the facts, and, of course, no one was prepared to deny them. In the second part of his speech, Peter makes an appeal based on the preceding facts (10, 11). It is very impressive, leaving his hearers no alternative. He says in effect, " We Jews were not saved by circumcision, so why should we impose this rite upon the Gentiles as a condition of salvation ? These were saved by grace, and we Jews can be saved in no other way.

No doubt Peter had talked over the whole subject with Paul, and had been finally convinced, if any doubt lingered in his mind after the Joppa-Caesarea experience, that Christianity was not a something added to Judaism, but was a new revelation and a Gospel. This address completely silenced the whole gathering (12a) and gave *Paul* and *Barnabas* a fine opportunity. They, made use of this, not by adding any argument to Peter's, but by simply *rehearsing what signs and wonders God had wrought among the Gentiles by them.* They illustrated the argument, and so greatly advanced the end they had in view. Barnabas' name precedes Paul's here, as the better known of the two, and as the leader of the Antioch party.

The Conference is proceeding very satisfactorily.

Thought : ALWAYS TAKE YOUR STAND ON FACTS.

THE ACTS xv. 13-21

Title : THE PRESIDENT SPEAKS

13 And after they had held their peace, James answered, saying,

Men and brethren, hearken unto me : 14 Simeon hath declared how God at the first did visit the Gentiles, to take out of them a people for his name. 15 And to this agree the words of the prophets ; as it is written, 16 After this I will return, and will build again the tabernacle of David, which is fallen down ; and I will build again the ruins thereof, and I will set it up : 17 That the residue of men might seek after the Lord, and all the Gentiles, upon whom my name is called, saith the Lord, who doeth all these things. 18 Known unto God are all his works from the beginning of the world. 19 Wherefore my sentence is, that we trouble not them, which from among the Gentiles are turned to God : 20 But that we write unto them, that they abstain from pollutions of idols, and from fornication, and from things strangled, and from blood. 21 For Moses of old time hath in every city them that preach him, being read in the synagogues every sabbath day.

EXPOSITION

Take time to be impressed by the fact that the chairman of this Conference, and bishop of Jerusalem, was one of Jesus' brothers. All through those Nazareth years, and after Jesus became a Rabbi, his brothers did not believe on Him, that is, they did not see in Him the promised Messiah (John vii. 5), and yet, within twenty years, this brother is not only a Christian, but is head of the mother church, and has written a New Testament Epistle. Jesus his brother is now his Lord (Jas. i. 1). Think about that! Well, he has listened carefully to all that has been said, and it is now his turn to speak. Chrysostom says, " This (James) was bishop, as they say, and, therefore, he speaks last."

Like Peter's speech, what James has to say falls into two parts. The first of these (14–18), deals with the main question at issue.

He begins by referring to Peter's speech, and he does so approvingly (14 R.V.) *" First"* corresponds to the *" good while ago"* of verse 7. *" To take out of them,"* means *" contrived to take," " looked out how he might take"* from among the Gentiles a people to be called by His name. That God had done this, Peter, Barnabas and Paul had shown. James, however, does not simply accept the fact, but shows that this very thing had been predicted, and more than once, as *" prophets"* intimates. Of such predictions he selects one, Amos ix. 11, 12, with a line added from Isaiah xlv. 21.

Look carefully at this quotation in conjunction with what Peter has said, for the point of the passage may easily be missed. James does not mean that the calling of the Gentiles, of which his brethren had been speaking, was the building again of David's fallen tabernacle. On the contrary, he says that that rebuilding was to follow this calling; *" after these things"* (16). There has been no greater blunder made in the interpretation of Old Testament prophecy than that which regards the Kingdom predictions as being fulfilled now in the Church. This passage gives no countenance to such a view. James speaks of Christians, Israelites and Gentiles. The

Christians are the Gentiles whom God is now calling out, and who are in His Church ; the Israelites are " *the residue of men*," of verse 17a, and the Gentiles are the nations who, in a day yet to come, shall turn unto the Lord (cf. Mic. iv. 2 ; Zech. viii. 21, 22). This statement of the bishop's brings the several parts of the Divine plan into relations with one-another, and shows that Christianity is not a developed Judaism.

That having been said on the main question, he now addresses himself to the immediate circumstance. How does the case of Gentile Christians stand, and what policy is to be pursued in the future ? In giving his judgment James speaks for the whole Church, and his verdict is masterly in conception and expression. He recognised that the Jews had a claim as well as the Gentiles, and that it would not be fair to give everything to either the one or the other, and so he proposes a middle course. He would not have the Gentiles " *troubled* " with the Mosaic ceremonialism, he would not have imposed on them the " *yoke* " which Peter had said the Jews themselves were *not able to bear* (10) ; but, on the other hand, they must so conduct themselves as not to outrage Jewish sensitiveness on certain matters of observance. He suggests that a letter be written, setting forth this verdict for the guidance of both elements in the Christian Church.

What the reservations were, we shall see in the following exposition.

Thought : CULTIVATE SANITY OF JUDG-MENT

THE ACTS xv. 22—35

Title : THE CHURCH'S FIRST LETTER

22 Then it pleased the apostles and elders, with the whole church, to send chosen men of their own company to Antioch with Paul and Barnabas ;

namely, Judas surnamed Barsabas, and Silas, chief men among the brethren : 23 And they wrote letters by them after this manner ;

THE APOSTLES AND ELDERS AND BRETHREN SEND GREETINGS UNTO THE BRETHREN WHICH ARE OF THE GENTILES IN ANTIOCH AND SYRIA AND CILICIA : 24 FORASMUCH AS WE HAVE HEARD, THAT CERTAIN WHICH WENT OUT FROM US HAVE TROUBLED YOU WITH WORDS, SUBVERTING YOUR SOULS, SAYING, YE MUST BE CIRCUMCISED, AND KEEP THE LAW : TO WHOM WE GAVE NO SUCH COMMANDMENT : 25 IT SEEMED GOOD UNTO US, BEING ASSEMBLED WITH ONE ACCORD, TO SEND CHOSEN MEN UNTO YOU WITH OUR BELOVED BARNABAS AND PAUL, 26 MEN THAT HAVE HAZARDED THEIR LIVES FOR THE NAME OF OUR LORD JESUS CHRIST. 27 WE HAVE SENT THEREFORE JUDAS AND SILAS, WHO SHALL ALSO TELL YOU THE SAME THINGS BY MOUTH. 28 FOR IT SEEMED GOOD TO THE HOLY GHOST, AND TO US, TO LAY UPON YOU NO GREATER BURDEN THAN THESE NECESSARY THINGS ; 29 THAT YE ABSTAIN FROM MEATS OFFERED TO IDOLS, AND FROM BLOOD, AND FROM THINGS STRANGLED, AND FROM FORNICATION : FROM WHICH IF YE KEEP YOURSELVES, YE SHALL DO WELL. FARE YE WELL.

30 So when they were dismissed, they came to Antioch : and when they had gathered the multitude together, they delivered the epistle : 31 Which when they had read, they rejoiced for the consolation. 32 And Judas and Silas, being prophets also themselves, exhorted the brethren with many words, and confirmed them. 33 And after they had tarried there a space, they were let go in peace from the brethren unto the apostles. 34 Notwithstanding it pleased Silas to abide there still. 35 Paul also and Barnabas continued in Antioch, teaching and preaching the word of the Lord, with many others also.

EXPOSITION

Having discussed thoroughly this Gentile matter, it was now resolved that a deputation be sent to Antioch, with a letter which would put their minds at rest who were troubled about the attitude of the

Judaizers. Two men, Silas and Judas, were chosen by " *the whole Church*," to accompany Paul and Barnabas.

The letter was drafted under the immediate direction of James, it would appear, for only once again in the New Testament does the salutation " *Greeting* " occur, and that is in James i. 1.

This is the first Epistle of the Christian Church, and its importance is out of all proportion to its length. Read it carefully, and mark the *Salutaton* (23), the *Repudiation* (24), the *Commendation* (25–27), the *Decrees* (28–29) and the *Conclusion* (29).

Do not overlook that expression in the *Salutation*, " *the brethren which are of the Gentiles.*" That registers a tremendous stride forward towards the realization of what we call the Holy Catholic Church, towards the enjoyment of that fellowship which rises high above all racial and social distinctions. Christian Gentiles are now regarded as parts of one indivisible Church, together with Christian Jews.

The *Repudiation* is impressive. The Church takes no responsibility either for the visit to Antioch of " *certain men* " (1), Jews, or for what they had said when they got there (24). They had " *troubled* " these Gentiles " *with words.*" What a lot of trouble words can give, and what a lot of help ! A dictionary never yet hurt any one, but selections from it have broken many a heart. Watch and winnow your words.

The *Commendation* is very hearty. One can feel the warmth of the words, " *our beloved Barnabas and Paul,*" and can appreciate the justice as well as the generosity of the acknowledgment of the risks they had taken for love of Christ and the souls of men. We should not withhold praise when and where it is due. We are generally very generous with blame.

Judas and Silas are given ample authority, and, when they read the letter to the Church in Antioch, and commented on it, they would be listened to with respect and eagerness (27).

It is noteworthy that in this letter of one hundred and nine words (Greek), only thirty-one deal with the matter in hand (28, 29). We can frustrate a purpose by too great emphasis : there is power in restraint.

And now mark carefully what is called "*The Decrees*" (xvi. 4). They are introduced by the assumption that the verdict of the Jerusalem Church is the verdict of the Holy Spirit, that He and they, that they and He came to this decision. They had taken upon themselves the duty of determining what the mind of the Spirit was. This must have been done by discussion and prayer together, and it was done by *the whole Church*, and not by a Clerical Council. Bishop Wordsworth wisely says, " It cannot be held that councils of the Church now are entitled to adopt the words of the text in the framing of canons." But, we must add, the Church has still the right to expect the guidance of the Holy Spirit in all her affairs.

And now for *the Decrees*. Four abstentions are enjoined. The Gentiles must abstain:

> " from things sacrificed to idols,
>   from blood,
>   from things strangled,
>   from fornication."

The first three concern ceremonial purity, and were of temporary importance, but the fourth concerns moral purity, and is of abiding obligation.

The first prohibition relates to food polluted by use at idol sacrifices, which was sent from the temples to the markets, and there bought and eaten. The second, " *blood*," relates to the drinking of it ; the third, is akin to this, but refers to blood which has not been " poured out " : for both matters read Lev. xvii. 10–13. The fourth prohibition needs no explanation, further than to say that idol-worship and fornication have always been closely connected.

Looking again at these *Decrees* we cannot but appreciate the wisdom with which this difficult and delicate matter was satisfactorily composed. The scruples of both parties had to be respected, and, by this settlement, were respected. The Pharisee party may well have said : " If we may not demand of Gentiles what would please us but be an offence to them (circumcision), let us forbid what may please them but be an offence to us (the four things." (Still)). That is the compromise which this letter embodies, and it was acceptable all round, and brought joy to the Gentiles (31).

Thinking again about this Conference and its issue, we cannot but realise how wonderfully so grave a crisis was negotiated. If the decision had been given to the Judaizers, Christianity, if it had survived, would have become a mere adjunct of Judaism. Think about that. And more than once in the history of the Church since those days, narrow-mindedness and bigotry would have imposed upon believers a burdensome yoke (10), nor has good council always prevailed. There are still people who think more of a symbol than of the reality, who are sticklers for forms of godliness while, all the time, they are denying the power.

We should learn from this Conference that it is well for brethren to confer, and endeavour to see one another's view-point, and well is it, also, that we should be willing, in the interests of Christian concord, to yield something, whenever we can do so without the sacrifice of principle. Temporary arrangements may make for peace. It is not to be expected that all Christians will ever see alike on all matters, nor is it desirable, but it is always possible, while holding our particular view, to have the fullest fellowship with those from whom we differ, only in the Holy Ghost (28). There can be no fellowship with wrong-doing.

Christianity is a religion of freedom and not of bondage, of peace, and not of strife, of love and not of ill-will. Is it that in you ?

Thought : *NO CHRISTIAN AND NO CHURCH HAS A MONOPOLY OF EITHER TRUTH OR WISDOM*

THE ACTS xv. 36—41

Title : *A REGRETTABLE INCIDENT*

36 And some days after, Paul said unto Barnabas, Let us go again and visit our brethren in every city where we have preached the word of the Lord, and see how they do. 37 And Barnabas determined to take with them John, whose surname was Mark. 38 But Paul thought not good to take him with them, who departed from them from Pamphylia, and went not with them to the work. 39 And the contention was so sharp between them, that they departed asunder one from the other : and so Barnabas took Mark, and sailed unto Cyprus ; 40 And Paul chose Silas and departed, being recommended by the brethren unto the grace of God. 41 And he went through Syria and Cilicia, confirming the churches.

EXPOSITION

The First Missionary Journey began in ch. xiii. 4, and ended in ch. xiv. 26. We are told that the returned missionaries " *tarried no little time* " with the disciples at Antioch. During this period the Jerusalem Conference was held, ch. xv. 1–35.

And now, Paul proposes a Second Missionary Journey (36), which he commences in verse 40.

But what concerns us here is what happened between the proposal and the start out. Paul and Barnabas parted company, men who had known each other for ten years, and had lived and served together for about six of these years; nor did they part company agreeably.

What was the trouble? John Mark. This young man had gone with Paul and Barnabas on the first missionary journey, and in the capacity of "*attendant*" (xiii. 5), or assistant. In exactly what way he assisted them we are not told, but Paul especially would need some one to help him in many ways. However, when the party reached Perga in Pamphylia, the place of first contact with Asia Minor, "*John departed from them and returned to Jerusalem*" (xiii. 13). This action is spoken of here by Luke as a *withdrawal* (38), and the word is *apostanta*, he apostatised. A terrible thing it is, indeed, for a young man and a Christian, to have that said about him. Why he left the party is not recorded, but Luke's "*withdrew*," and "*went not with them to the work*," denote decided blame. Perhaps Mark's courage failed him; perhaps there was a change of plan, relative to the course they should take, perhaps Mark had more sympathy with Peter's conservatism than with Paul's liberalism; perhaps these, and other things combined, led to the deflection and defection. Anyhow, Mark was wrong.

And now, when Paul proposed a second journey, Barnabas, a cousin of Mark's (Col. iv. 10 R.V.) suggested that he should again accompany them. Paul, however, would not have it, and there was "*a sharp contention*" (*paroxusmos*), an angry dispute, a paroxysm between them. This resulted in their parting company, Barnabas taking Mark, and going to Cyprus (39, cf. iv. 36), and Paul taking Silas, and going again to Galatia (40, 36).

The question will inevitably arise, at this point, "Which of these two good and great men was right, and which wrong, in this dispute?" Observation, if not experience, teaches us that in affairs of this sort, rarely is one of the parties altogether wrong, and the other altogether right; generally, a measure of blame attaches to each, and generally, each is contending for a principle. It was so in this case, at any rate.

Paul owed much to Barnabas (ix. 26, 27), and Barnabas owed much to Paul, and surely they could have come to some amicable decision on this matter without quarrelling and separating. Each was contending for something that was worthy : Paul would have Mark know that the work of the Lord must not be treated in that way ; and Barnabas, who did not condone Mark's action, would give the young man a chance to retrieve his character. Both these purposes are worthy. Paul was intense, and Barnabas was kind, and each carried his virtue beyond the line of virtue. There are times when the Barnabas-like should be severe, and there are times when the Paul-like should be tender. No young man should be turned down for one mistake. There was good stuff in Mark, as subsequent events showed .

Chrysostom says that this strife was of great service to Mark, for the sternness of Paul brought a change in his mind, while the kindness of Barnabas suffered him not to feel abandoned. He made good at last, and Paul was reconciled. " *Take Mark, and bring him with thee ; for he is profitable to me for the ministry* " (2 Tim. iv. 11).

As we take leave of this story let us resolve that our tenderness shall not degenerate into softness, nor our severity into harshness.

Thought : THE STEP FROM GRACE TO DISGRACE CAN BE EASILY TAKEN

THE ACTS xvi. 1-13

Title : GOING WEST

1 Then came he to Derbe and Lystra : and, behold a certain disciple was there, named Timotheus, the son of a certain woman, which was a Jewess, and

believed ; but his father was a Greek : 2 Which was
well reported of by the brethren that were at Lystra
and Iconium. 3 Him would Paul have to go forth
with him ; and took and circumcised him because of
the Jews which were in those quarters : for they
knew all that his father was a Greek. 4 And as they
went through the cities, they delivered them the
Decrees for to keep, that were ordained of the
apostles and elders which were at Jerusalem. 5 And
so were the churches established in the faith, and
increased in number daily.

6 Now when they had gone throughout Phrygia
and the region of Galatia, and were forbidden of the
Holy Ghost to preach the word in Asia, 7 After they
were come to Mysia, they assayed to go into Bithynia:
but the Spirit suffered them not. 8 And they passing by Mysia came down to Troas. 9 And a vision
appeared to Paul in the night ; There stood a man of
Macedonia, and prayed him, saying, Come over into
Macedonia, and help us. 10 And after he had seen
the vision, immediately we endeavoured to go into
Macedonia, assuredly gathering that the Lord had
called us for to preach the gospel unto them.

11 Therefore loosing from Troas, we came with
a straight course to Samothracia, and the next day
to Neapolis ; 12 And from thence to Philippi, which
is the chief city of that part of Macedonia, and a
colony : and we were in that city abiding certain days.
13 And on the sabbath we went out of the city by a
river side, where prayer was wont to be made ; and
we sat down, and spake unto the women which resorted thither.

EXPOSITION

Paul's *Second Tour* (xv. 40 to xviii. 22) belongs
to A.D. 51–54, and was in three distinct fields.

1. IN ASIA MINOR (xv. 36 to xvi, 10). The
geography of to-day's portion includes, S.C.D.L.P.G.
T.S.N.P., that is, from the Syrian Antioch to Philippi.
Look up the map. Here is Paul at Lystra again (1).
Danger seems to have an attraction for him, or was
it his love for his converts ? (1) Does verse 1 hide a
tragedy : a husband and wife of different nations

and faith, and one child! Mark might have had the place which was given to Timothy (xv. 38; xvi. 3). Paul had an object in choosing a man who was half a Gentile (3). " *The cities* " (4) were in the provinces of Phrygia and Galatia (6).

The *Vision* vouchsafed at Troas ushered in the most momentous event in the history of Europe, the going forth of the Gospel to enlighten the nations of the West. Paul and his company intended, evidently, to go in the direction of Ephesus from Pisidia, but this was not allowed, the Holy Spirit forbidding them (6). They then turned north, and would have entered the province of Bithynia, but here again their way was blocked (7), so they turned westward to Troas, where positive direction was given to them (8–10). This is a great passage on Divine Guidance. Bithynia was for Peter, not for Paul (7, with 1 Pet. i. 1). There's a place for each of us. The " *we* " sections in the " Acts " are those which include Luke, and as the first of them begins at verse 10 it is clear that Luke joined Paul at Troas, and, in all likelihood, is the " *man of Macedonia* " of verse 9. Observe carefully the use of the pronouns from now on. " *We* " is dropped when Paul left Philippi (xvii. 1), and reappears when he returned to that city (xx. 2, 5), so that, in all likelihood, Luke was left in charge of the church there. " *Come over, and help us* " (9). Have you ever heard that cry? And have you " *endeavoured to go ?* " (10).

Thought : THERE IS NO VENTURE WHERE THERE'S NO VISION (9, 10).

THE ACTS xvi. 14-24

Title : CHRISTIAN CONQUESTS

14 And a certain woman named Lydia, a seller of purple, of the city of Thyatira, which worshipped God, heard us : whose heart the Lord opened, that she attended unto the things which were spoken of Paul. 15 And when she was baptised, and her household, she besought us, saying, If ye have judged me to be faithful to the Lord, come into my house, and abide there. And she constrained us.

16 And it came to pass, as we went to prayer, a certain damsel possessed with a spirit of divination met us, which brought her masters much gain by soothsaying : 17 The same followed Paul and us, and cried, saying, These men are the servants of the most high God, which shew unto us the way of salvation. 18 And this did she many days. But Paul, being grieved, turned and said to the spirit, I command thee in the name of Jesus Christ to come out of her. And he came out the same hour.

19 And when her masters saw that the hope of their gains was gone, they caught Paul and Silas, and drew them into the marketplace unto the rulers, 20 And brought them to the magistrates, saying, These men, being Jews, do exceedingly trouble our city, 21 And teach customs, which are not lawful for us to receive, neither to observe, being Romans. 22 And the multitude rose up together against them: and the magistrates rent off their clothes, and commanded to beat them. 23 And when they had laid many stripes upon them, they cast them into prison, charging the jailor to keep them safely : 24 Who, having received such a charge, thrust them into the inner prison, and made their feet fast in the stocks.

EXPOSITION

2. In Macedonia (xvi. 11 to xvii. 15). Paul, Silas and Luke are now at Philippi. In all likelihood it was Luke's place of residence. He here narrates some of the experiences of his companions in this city. These relate to a *woman*, a *girl*, and a *man*. From what is told of these, we may say that the woman represents *Asiatic commerce ;* the girl, *Greek slavery ;* and the man, *Roman government.* We are given to see the impact of Christianity upon each of these ; and each time it was victorious. Look at these cases.

122

(i) THE WOMAN (13–15). She is the first Christian convert made in Europe, and a most important part of the work of Christianity in Europe has been the elevation of woman. The beginnings at Philippi were inauspicious. When the Sabbath arrived there was no synagogue to which the Jews and the missionaries could go. Was the day then, to be lost ? Oh, no. A few women, Jewesses, or proselytes, were in the habit of assembling for prayer on the banks of the Gangas, and the missionaries joined them. Because we cannot do all that we would, is no reason for our not doing all that we can. That morning a convert was secured. Mark all that is said about her ; the woman of the open heart and the open house.

(ii) THE GIRL (16–24). Here is a pitched battle between truth and error, between love and selfishness. A girl with an evil spirit is being exploited for gain by a number of men. The demon is exorcised ; a tumult arises ; a charge is preferred ; no trial is held, but Paul and Silas are thrown into jail. This is a purely *Gentile* persecution, and the first in Europe. There never has been a time when Christianity has been unchallenged, and generally, when most fiercely assailed it has been most successful. Christianity thrives, not in a hot house, but in the open and before the blast. Is your Christianity virile, and vigorous, and victorious ?

Thought : IT IS BETTER TO BOW TO TRUTH THAN TO BE BROKEN BY IT.

THE ACTS xvi. 25-40

Title : A CONCERT IN A CELL

25 And at midnight Paul and Silas prayed, and sang praises unto God : and the prisoners heard them. 26 And suddenly there was a great earthquake, so that the foundations of the prison were shaken : and immediately all the doors were

opened, and every one's bands were loosed. 27 And the keeper of the prison awaking out of his sleep, and seeing the prison doors open, he drew out his sword, and would have killed himself, supposing that the prisoners had been fled. 28 But Paul cried with a loud voice, saying, Do thyself no harm : for we are all here. 29 Then he called for a light, and sprang in, and came trembling, and fell down before Paul and Silas, 30 And brought them out, and said, Sirs, what must I do to be saved ? 31 And they said, Believe on the Lord Jesus Christ, and thou shalt be saved, and thy house. 32 And they spake unto him the word of the Lord, and to all that were in his house. 33 And he took them the same hour of the night, and washed their stripes : and was baptized, he and all his, straightway. 34 And when he had brought them into his house, he set meat before them, and rejoiced, believing in God with all his house.

35 And when it was day, the magistrates sent the serjeants, saying, Let those men go. 36 And the keeper of the prison told this saying to Paul, The magistrates have sent to let you go : now therefore depart, and go in peace. 37 But Paul said unto them, They have beaten us openly uncondemned, being Romans, and have cast us into prison ; and now do they thrust us out privily ? nay verily ; but let them come themselves and fetch us out. 38 And the serjeants told these words unto the magistrates : and they feared, when they heard that they were Romans. 39 And they came and besought them, and brought them out, and desired them to depart out of the city. 40 And they went out of the prison, and entered into the house of Lydia : and when they had seen the brethren, they comforted them, and departed.

EXPOSITION

(iii) THE MAN (25–40). This is a thrilling story. Prison, midnight, wounds, songs, earthquake, fear, contemplated suicide, conviction, inquiry, the Gospel, faith, kindness, confession, joy, remonstrance, release, consolation ; these are the notes of the story.

No suffering can still the Christian's song, and no night can hide his light. Christians are still singing their song in the night. These prisoners had an impromptu and free concert. Perhaps Paul would sing the ' air,' and Silas, the ' part.' I wonder if it was a psalm they sang ?

Well, there was a quake in the prison, and then in the jailor, but both were righted. Instead of the jailor keeping the prisoners, the prisoners saved the jailor (27, 28). " *He called for a light*," and he needed it badly. He might have had it earlier, for Christians " *are the light of the world*." Some people never think about *salvation* until they are threatened by death (30). Here is the simplest expression of the Gospel (31). A Christian service is held on the spot (32), and everybody is ' washed,' the stripes of the missionaries, and the sins of the jailor and his family (33). Look at these prisoners and their keeper having a gladsome and believing time together over a meal ! (34). The change in the jailor expressed itself at once in *love* and *joy*, and Paul has told us that these are part of the " fruit of the Spirit " (Gal. v. 22). Modernism has no such tale to tell.

When day dawned the rest of the drama unfolded itself. The authorities, who had heard the news, said that the prisoners might go (35, 36). But Paul said in effect, " not at all ; let them sup their own brew ; they have humbled us, now they shall humble themselves ; they attended personally to our degradation, and they shall attend personally to our vindication." And they did (37–39). Mark the contrasts here (37, 20) : " *publicly, privately*," " *cast out, conducted out*," and " *Jews, Romans*."

Because we are Christians, we are not to be soft. There is a meekness which is weakness. There should be iron in the Christian's blood. Don't be supine, but strong.

Thought : " STONE WALLS DO NOT A PRISON MAKE."

Title : REJECTED AND ACCEPTED

1 Now when they had passed through Amphipolis and Apollonia, they came to Thessalonica, where was a synagogue of the Jews : 2 And Paul, as his manner was, went in unto them, and three sabbath days reasoned with them out of the scriptures, 3 Opening and alleging, that Christ must needs have suffered, and risen again from the dead ; and that this Jesus, whom I preach unto you, is Christ 4 And some of them believed, and consorted with Paul and Silas ; and of the devout Greeks a great multitude, and of the chief women not a few.

5 But the Jews which believed not, moved with envy, took unto them certain lewd fellows of the baser sort, and gathered a company, and set all the city on an uproar, and assaulted the house of Jason, and sought to bring them out to the people. 6 And when they found them not, they drew Jason and certain brethren unto the rulers of the city, crying, These that have turned the world upside down are come hither also ; 7 Whom Jason hath received : and these all do contrary to the decrees of Cæsar, saying that there is another king, one Jesus. 8 And they troubled the people and the rulers of the city, when they heard these things. 9 And when they had taken security of Jason, and of the other, they let them go.

10 And the brethren immediately sent away Paul and Silas by night unto Berea : who coming thither went into the synagogue of the Jews. 11 These were more noble than those in Thessalonica, in that they received the word with all readiness of mind, and searched the scriptures daily, whether those things were so. 12 Therefore many of them believed ; also of honourable women which were Greeks, and of men, not a few. 13 But when the Jews of Thessalonica had knowledge that the word of God was preached of Paul at Berea, they came thither also, and stirred up the people. 14 And then immediately the brethren sent away Paul to go as it were to the sea : but Silas and Timotheus abode there still. 15 And they that

**conducted Paul brought him unto Athens : and
receiving a commandment unto Silas and Timotheus
for to come to him with all speed, they departed.**

EXPOSITION

We now see the end of the missionaries' labours,
for the present, in Macedonia. From Philippi the
places visited were—A.A.T.B. (1, 10).

AT THESSALONICA (1–9). This is the present
Salonika, about one hundred miles from Philippi.
With verses 2–4 read 1 Thess. i., with verses 5–9,
1 Thess ii., and with verse 10, 1 Thess. iii. Thessalonica
was the metropolis of the province of Macedonia,
its most populous city, and the most important town
so far visited by Paul on his missionary journeys.
For where, and what he preached there, see verses 2,
3, and 1, 2. Thess.

" *Three Sabbaths* " (2). Perhaps he gave one to
the *sufferings* of the Christ ; one, to His *resurrection*,
and one to demonstrate that *Jesus is the Christ*.
Compare the *women* here, and at Berea (4, 12) with
those of Antioch (xiii. 50). The currents of faith
and unbelief run side by side throughout this Book
(4, 5). *Jealousy* spreads itself like the plague (5).
Jason sheltered dangerous guests, and deserves great
honour (7). A little succour is worth more than a
lot of sympathy.

AT BEREA (10–14). Those who were " *let* go,"
" *sent away* " Paul and Silas (9, 10). Wherever they
went they were bent on preaching (10). We never
read of Paul doing any sight-seeing, and he gives us
practically no description of the ancient wonders he
must have looked upon. Truly did he say, " *one
thing I do.*" What is the evidence of true *nobility* ?
(11). We are here reminded of the duty of individual
research (11). Do you *search the Scriptures daily* ?
(11). The Jews *stirred up the people* for the devil
(13), but the missionaries *turned up the world* for the
Lord (6). A world which is downside up, needs to be
turned up side down. This whole story is " a moving

scene," moving from place to place. There is nothing stagnant about the Gospel. Christianity is necessarily propagating.

Thought : THERE IS NOTHING SO THRILLING AS THE MISSIONARY ENTERPRISE.

THE ACTS xvii. 16-34

Title : PAUL AMONG THE PHILOSOPHERS

16 Now while Paul waited for them at Athens, his spirit was stirred in him, when he saw the city wholly given to idolatry. 17 Therefore disputed he in the synagogue with the Jews, and with the devout persons, and in the market daily with them that met with him. 18 Then certain philosophers of the Epicureans, and of the Stoicks, encountered him. And some said, What will this babbler say? other some, He seemeth to be a setter forth of strange gods : because he preached unto them Jesus, and the resurrection. 19 And they took him, and brought him unto Areopagus, saying, May we know what this new doctrine, whereof thou speakest, is? 20 For thou bringest certain strange things to our ears : we would know therefore what these things mean. 21 (For all the Athenians and strangers which were there spent their time in nothing else, but either to tell, or to hear some new thing.) 22 Then Paul stood in the midst of Mars' hill, and said,

Ye men of Athens, I perceive that in all things ye are too superstitious. 23 For as I passed by, and beheld your devotions, I found an altar with this inscription, TO THE UNKNOWN GOD. Whom therefore ye ignorantly worship, him declare I unto you. 24 God that made the world and all things therein, seeing that he is Lord of heaven and earth, dwelleth not in temples made with hands ; 25 Neither is worshipped with men's hands, as though he needed any thing, seeing he giveth to all life, and breath, and all things ; 26 And hath made of one blood all nations of men for to dwell on all the face of the earth, and hath determined the times before appointed, and the bounds of their habitation; 27 That they should seek the Lord, if haply they might feel after him, and find him, though he be not far from every one of us: 28 For in him we live, and move, and have our being; as certain also of your own poets have said,

For we are also his offspring.

29 Forasmuch then as we are the offspring of God, we ought not to think that the Godhead is like unto gold, or silver, or stone, graven by art and man's device. 30 And the times of this ignorance God winked at; but now commandeth all men every where to repent: 31 Because he hath appointed a day, in the which he will judge the world in righteousness by that man whom he hath ordained; whereof he hath given assurance unto all men, in that he hath raised him from the dead.

32 And when they heard of the resurrection of the dead, some mocked: and others said, We will hear thee again of this matter. 33 So Paul departed from among them. 34 Howbeit certain men clave unto him, and believed: among the which was Dionysius the Areopagite, and a woman named Damaris, and others with them.

EXPOSITION

3. IN ACHAIA (xvii. 16 to xviii. 22). This is a momentous passage, treating, as it does of, THE FOUNDATIONS OF RELIGION. Mark these paragraphs —(a) THE OCCASION (16–21), (b) THE DISCOURSE (22–31). (c) THE RESULT (32–34).

(a) THE OCCASION. *Paul was waiting for his companions:* all alone, yet not alone. *He was surveying the Grecian capital.* Mark the spectacle he beheld, and the feelings it aroused. *He was disputing with the Athenian citizens;* in the synagogue with the Jews, and in the Agora with the heathen. Paul did more while he waited than some folk do when they are working (16). It was not the *sights* in ATHENS, but the *souls* that attracted Paul (16);

he was not a tourist, but a missionary, and preached both indoors and out (17). What a scene this is— PAUL AMONG THE PHILOSOPHERS, the greatest man that ever stood on Mars' Hill (18–21). What will he do with such an opportunity? for, let us remember, opportunity, if it has made some, has marred others.

(b) THE DISCOURSE. After an introduction, brief, but very tactful (22, 23), Paul delivers one of the greatest messages of his ministry. Here is the Outline. *The Pleasing Introduction*, with its respectful salutation, and its complimentary ascription (22). *The Pathetic Inscription*, with its tactful intimation, and startling declaration (23). *The Profound Interpretation*, revealing God in His manifold relations. 1. GOD AND THE UNIVERSE (24, 25). 1. *The Facts.* 2. *The Teaching.*

II. GOD AND THE RACE (26–29). 1. *His Relation to the Race Collectively* (26, 27a), revealing *Transcendence.* 2. *His Relation to the Race Individually* (27b, 28), revealing *Immanence.* 3. *The Teaching Resulting from these Truths* (29).

III. GOD AND THE AGES (30, 31). 1. *His Relation to the Past Ages.* (30a). 2. *His Relation to the Present Age* (30b, 31). Only weeks of study will reveal the sweep and power of this discourse. Some think that this message was Paul's great mistake: that he pandered to philosophy, and so, failed. I do not accept that view. Did he fail?

(c) THE RESULT (32–34). Some mocked; some procrastinated; and some believed (32). Is not that always the result of Gospel preaching? SOCRATES is to-day of antiquarian interest, but CHRIST is the living issue. What is your attitude towards Him? Division? delay? or decision?

Thought: SOME DEFEATS ARE ONLY IN-
STALMENTS OF VICTORY.

Title : *PAUL AT CORINTH*

1 After these things Paul departed from Athens, and came to Corinth ; 2 And found a certain Jew named Aquila, born in Pontus, lately come from Italy, with his wife Priscilla ; (because that Claudius had commanded all Jews to depart from Rome :) and came unto them. 3 And because he was of the same craft, he abode with them, and wrought : for by their occupation they were tentmakers. 4 And he reasoned in the synagogue every sabbath, and persuaded the Jew and the Greeks.

5 And when Silas and Timotheus were come from Macedonia, Paul was pressed in the spirit, and testified to the Jews that Jesus was Christ. 6 And when they opposed themselves, and blasphemed, he shook his raiment, and said unto them, Your blood be upon your own heads ; I am clean : from henceforth I will go unto the Gentiles. 7 And he departed thence, and entered into a certain man's house, named Justus, one that worshipped God, whose house joined hard to the synagogue. 8 And Crispus, the chief ruler of the synagogue, believed on the Lord with all his house ; and many of the Corinthians hearing believed, and were baptized. 9 Then spake the Lord to Paul in the night by a vision, Be not afraid, but speak, and hold not thy peace : 10 For I am with thee, and no man shall set on thee to hurt thee : for I have much people in this city. 11 And he continued there a year and six months, teaching the word of God among them.

12 And when Gallio was the deputy of Achaia, the Jews made insurrection with one accord against Paul, and brought him to the judgment seat, 13 Saying, This fellow persuadeth men to worship God contrary to the law. 14 And when Paul was now about to open his mouth, Gallio said unto the Jews, If it were a matter of wrong or wicked lewdness, O ye Jews, reason would that I should bear with you : 15 But if it be a question of words and names, and of your law, look ye to it ; for I will be no judge of such matters. 16 And he drave them from the judgment seat. 17 Then all the Greeks took

Sosthenes, the chief ruler of the synagogue, and beat him before the judgment seat. And Gallio cared for none of those things.

EXPOSITION

The Second Missionary Journey is drawing to a close. Paul is still in ACHAIA, and now in its capital, CORINTH, which stood on the great highway between East and West. It possessed two harbours, one connecting its trade with Asia, and the other, with Italy and the West ; and it was a city of abysmal profligacy. Corinth, therefore, was a model sphere for missionary labour, wherein the adaptation of the Gospel to all classes of Society was put to the test, and also, wherein the relation of Christian principles to every aspect of life might be demonstrated. Paul was here for eighteen months (11) in the years A.D. 52–54. Thinking of his work in this place, we should mark its *beginning* (1–4), its *progress* (5–8), and its *result* (9–17).

1. The *Beginning* is impressive. Going from Athens to Corinth, was like going from Oxford or Cambridge to London. Paul arrives alone (1), makes two friends (2), and works with them at tent-making to earn a living (3), employing his week-ends by preaching (4). He was in actual want at this time (2 Cor. xi. 9). Never judge of the end of a thing by the beginning.

2. The *Progress* is checkered. Paul's message is clearer and more direct than ever (1 Cor. ii. 2), but it is evident that he was working under intense nervous strain, and was very depressed (5 ; 1 Cor. ii. 3). Jesus, at times, was depressed. Does that thought help you at all ? Paul turns from the Jews to the Gentiles, and the Christian meeting-house was next door to the Synagogue (6, 7). Awkward ! Some of the Jews walked out of the one into the other : and didn't ask for a transfer (8) !

3. The *Result* is summarized. When Paul had

132

nearly lost heart, the Lord came to him. Mark the double exhortation and double encouragement (9, 10). During this eighteen months (11), Paul wrote 1 Thessalonians in A.D. 52 ; and 2 Thessalonians in A.D. 53. Read them here. In what follows (12-17) mark the relation of Legalism (12, 13), Secularism (14-16), and Heathenism (17) to the Gospel.

Thought : WHEN YOU ARE DOWN IN THE
DUMPS, THE LORD IS AT HAND.

THE ACTS xviii. 18-28

Title : APOLLOS THE ORATOR

18 And Paul after this tarried there yet a good while, and then took his leave of the brethren, and sailed thence into Syria, and with him Priscilla and Aquila ; having shorn his head in Cenchrea : for he had a vow. 19 And he came to Ephesus, and left them there : but he himself entered into the synagogue, and reasoned with the Jews. 20 When they desired him to tarry longer time with them, he consented not ; 21 But bade them farewell, saying, I must by all means keep this feast that cometh in Jerusalem : but I will return again unto you, if God will. And he sailed from Ephesus.

22 And when he had landed at Cæsarea, and gone up, and saluted the church, he went down to Antioch. 23 And after he had spent some time there, he departed, and went over all the country of Galatia and Phrygia in order, strengthening all the disciples.

24 And a certain Jew named Apollos, born at Alexandria, an eloquent man, and mighty in the scriptures, came to Ephesus. 25 This man was instructed in the way of the Lord ; and being fervent in the spirit, he spake and taught diligently the things of the Lord, knowing only the baptism of John. 26 And he began to speak boldly in the synagogue : whom when Aquila and Priscilla had heard, they took him unto them, and expounded

133

unto him the way of God more perfectly. **27** And when he was disposed to pass into Achaia, the brethren wrote, exhorting the disciples to receive him : who, when he was come, helped them much which had believed through grace : **28** For he mightily convinced the Jews, and that publickly, shewing by the scriptures that Jesus was Christ.

EXPOSITION

How amazingly compressed is the record in verses 18–22. Try and imagine all that they mean. The line of Churches which Paul had planted from east to west was broken by the province of Asia, of which EPHESUS was the metropolis ; and this narrative tells us how the gap was filled. Why had Paul left the gap ? (xvi. 6). Study a map. The places visited by Paul, from his entering Achaia to his arrival again at his missionary base, were— A.C.C.E.C.J.A. Take time to be impressed by this spread of the Gospel, and Paul's policy of planting it in strategic centres : ANTIOCH, PHILIPPI, CORINTH, EPHESUS ; and more to follow.

During this brief visit to Ephesus the foundation of a vigorous and flourishing church was laid. Much can be done in a short time when one is filled with the Holy Spirit. Was it right for Paul to avow ? (18). The best of people are not infallible. Compare xxi. 24, and the result.

THE THIRD MISSIONARY JOURNEY (xviii. 23 to xxi. 14) ; A.D. 54–58. We are now to consider Christian activities in ASIA and EUROPE. It is noteworthy that Luke here summarizes in a single verse (23) a great amount of work which Paul did. How unlike evangelists who write columns about every mission they hold ! But the historian goes into detail about another preacher, a striking personality. APOLLOS was an Alexandrian Jew, a man of ability, culture, and eloquence. We first meet with him at Ephesus, like a blazing comet in the ecclesiastical heavens, striking down opposition and

134

unbelief with the onslaught of his fervid and logical eloquence (24–26a). Unlike most people of his ability, he was teachable (26b). The man who has finished his education never began it. Nobody knows all that the Bible has to teach ; and we all may learn much from those who cannot wield our influence. Notice the nature of this man's ministry in Ephesus (25) and in Corinth (27, 28). Read 1 Cor. i. to iii, thinking of Apollos. Perhaps he wrote the Epistle to the HEBREWS.

Thought : *IF WE CANNOT BE GREAT OUR-SELVES, WE MAY HELP THOSE WHO ARE* (26).

THE ACTS xix. 1-12

Title : *THE BEGINNING OF A GREAT MINISTRY*

1 And it came to pass, that, while Apollos was at Corinth, Paul having passed through the upper coasts came to Ephesus : and finding certain disciples, 2 He said unto them, Have ye received the Holy Ghost since ye believed ? And they said unto him, We have not so much as heard whether there be any Holy Ghost. 3 And he said unto them, Unto what then were ye baptized ? And they said, Unto John's baptism. 4 Then said Paul, John verily baptized with the baptism of repentance, saying unto the people, that they should believe on him which should come after him, that is, on Christ Jesus. 5 When they heard this, they were baptized in the name of the Lord Jesus. 6 And when Paul had laid his hands upon them, the Holy Ghost came on them ; and they spake with tongues, and prophesied. 7 And all the men were about twelve.

8 And he went into the synagogue, and spake boldly for the space of three months, disputing and persuading the things concerning the kingdom of God. 9 But when divers were hardened, and

believed not, but spake evil of that way before the multitude, he departed from them, and separated the disciples, disputing daily in the school of one Tyrannus. 10 And this continued by the space of two years; so that all they which dwelt in Asia heard the word of the Lord Jesus, both Jews and Greeks. 11 And God wrought special miracles by the hands of Paul: 12 So that from his body were brought unto the sick handkerchiefs or aprons, and the diseases departed from them, and the evil spirits went out of them.

EXPOSITION

Recall exactly where we are in the unfolding of this wonderful story. Division III. of the Book: THE GENTILE PERIOD OF THE CHURCH'S WITNESS (chs. xiii. to xxviii.). 1. PAUL'S TIRELESS ACTIVITIES (xiii. 1 to xxi. 16). (iii) HIS THIRD MISSIONARY JOURNEY (xviii. 23 to xxi. 16).

Paul, who had gone "*over all the country of Galatia and Phrygia*" (xviii. 23), now comes to EPHESUS (xix. 1), where he remained for *three years* (xx. 31). This is his second visit in A.D. 54 (18, 19), and he remained until A.D. 57, and in this great centre firmly did he plant the standard of the Cross in Asia. Glance over the letters to the Seven Asian Churches (Rev. ii., iii.): also read *Ephesians* and *Colossians*.

Our first paragraph relates to (a) *Progressive Revelation and Apprehension* (1–7). These men (7) were, no doubt, Jews, synagogue worshippers, and with some knowledge of, and faith in, Jesus Christ: probably they were converts of Apollos (xviii. 21–26). Be sure to read verse 2 in R.V. We should remember to distinguish between *life* and *light* divine. There cannot be the latter without the former, but there may be the former and very little of the latter, as in the case before us. Apprehension as well as revelation is progressive. JOHN'S BAPTISM had in view *a coming Deliverer*; CHRISTIAN BAPTISM has in view *a present*

Saviour. The one was evidence of repentance ; the other, of regeneration. These men were baptized twice (4, 5). Christian baptism can be nothing other than the baptism of Christians.

The next paragraph tells of (b) *Triumphs of the Gospel at Ephesus* (8–20). Mark these points : for three months Paul exercised his ministry in the synagogue ; the majority opposed the Word ; Paul separated the Jewish believers, and formed a Christian Assembly in Ephesus ; this became the centre from which he evangelized Proconsular Asia ; God bore him witness by enabling him to perform " *special powers* " (8–12). The Christian Gospel has always been a testing and dividing energy, and will be to the end. There are times when separation from religious associations is justifiable (9). Christianity is eternally " THE WAY " (9). We must *reason* if we would *persuade* (8).

Thought : ADVANCE IN AND WITH CHRIST

THE ACTS xix. 13-27

Title : TRICKERY TROUNCED

13 Then certain of the vagabond Jews, exorcists, took upon them to call over them which had evil spirits the name of the Lord Jesus, saying, We adjure you by Jesus whom Paul preacheth. 14 And there were seven sons of one Sceva, a Jew, and chief of the priests, which did so. 15 And the evil spirit answered and said, Jesus I know, and Paul I know ; but who are ye ? 16 And the man in whom the evil spirit was leaped on them, and overcame them, and prevailed against them, so that they fled out of that house naked and wounded. 17 And this was known to all the Jews and Greeks also dwelling at Ephesus ; and fear fell on them all, and the name of the Lord Jesus was magnified. 18 And many that believed came, and confessed, and shewed their deeds. 19 Many of them also which used curious arts

137

brought their books together, and burned them before all men : and they counted the price of them, and found it fifty thousand pieces of silver. 20 So mightily grew the word of God and prevailed.

21 After these things were ended, Paul purposed in the spirit, when he had passed through Macedonia and Achaia, to go to Jerusalem, saying, After I have been there, I must also see Rome. 22 So he sent into Macedonia two of them that ministered unto him, Timotheus and Erastus ; but he himself stayed in Asia for a season.

23 And the same time there arose no small stir about that way. 24 For a certain man named Demetrius, a silversmith, which made silver shrines for Diana, brought no small gain unto the craftsmen : 25 Whom he called together with the workmen of like occupation, and said, Sirs, ye know that by this craft we have our wealth. 26 Moreover ye see and hear, that not alone at Ephesus, but almost throughout all Asia, this Paul hath persuaded and turned away much people, saying that they be no gods, which are made with hands : 27 So that not only this our craft is in danger to be set at nought ; but also that the temple of the great goddess Diana should be despised, and her magnificence should be destroyed, whom all Asia and the world worshippeth.

EXPOSITION

The Gospel necessarily must come into collision with every form of evil. Here it collides with magic and trickery, much to the humiliation of the latter. Observe two things.

1. THE CARNAL AND THE SPIRITUAL (13–17). Here, consider carefully the *presumption*, the *exposure*, the *judgment*, and the *result*. Christianity is always a challenge : it throws down the gauntlet to every would-be rival, and it always tests its strength in the open. And it is always victorious, proved by preaching (8), perversity (10), persistence (10), power (11, 12), pretence (13–16), and progress (17–20). Special attention should be given to verse 15, where

two Greek words are translated "*know*." Para-phrased it reads, "The Jesus whom you invoke is one whose authority *I acknowledge*; and the Paul whom you name *I recognize* to be the servant or messenger of God; but what sort of men are ye, who have been empowered to act as you do by neither?" (Lindsay). That's pretty good for a demon. The fact is, spiritual warfare cannot be waged with carnal weapons. God's work must be done by God's people, in God's way, for God's glory. Christ never asked for Caesar's acknowledgment or aid, and why should He? Wealthy, ungodly chairmen for religious meetings! Dance-floors to attract our youth to Church! Raffles to prevent a deficit on Church accounts! Away with this Laodiceanism.

2. THE SIGNS OF SINCERITY (18–20). Mark here the conjunction of *faith, confession, sacrifice,* and *prosperity*. They cannot be separated. When one really *believes*, he will own up to wrong in his life, and then, at all costs, he will put that wrong away. These magical formulæ were worth anything from £2,000 to £6,000. But the souls of these people were worth infinitely more. Mark, they did not *sell* these "books," they *burnt* them. When you abandon what is wrong in your life, do not give it to some one else, for, or without, money; turn it into smoke, and it will come back to you in refreshing rain.

Thought: *REALITY CANNOT FOR LONG BE COUNTERFEITED.*

THE ACTS xix. 28-41

Title: *A STORM IN A TEA-CUP*

28 And when they heard these sayings, they were full of wrath, and cried out, saying, Great is Diana of the Ephesians. 29 And the whole city was filled with confusion: and having caught Gaius and Aristarchus, men of Macedonia, Paul's companions

in travel, they rushed with one accord into the theatre. 30 And when Paul would have entered in unto the people, the disciples suffered him not. 31 And certain of the chief of Asia, which were his friends, sent unto him, desiring him that he would not adventure himself into the theatre. 32 Some therefore cried one thing, and some another : for the assembly was confused ; and the more part knew not wherefore they were come together. 33 And they drew Alexander out of the multitude, the Jews putting him forward. And Alexander beckoned with the hand, and would have made his defence unto the people. 34 But when they knew that he was a Jew, all with one voice about the space of two hours cried out, Great is Diana of the Ephesians. 35 And when the townclerk had appeased the people, he said,

Ye men of Ephesus, what man is there that knoweth not how that the city of the Ephesians is a worshipper of the great goddess Diana, and of the image which fell down from Jupiter ? 36 Seeing then that these things cannot be spoken against, ye ought to be quiet, and to do nothing rashly. 37 For ye have brought hither these men, which are neither robbers of churches, nor yet blasphemers of your goddess. 38 Wherefore if Demetrius, and the craftsmen which are with him, have a matter against any man, the law is open, and there are deputies : let them implead one another. 39 But if ye enquire any thing concerning other matters, it shall be determined in a lawful assembly. 40 For we are in danger to be called in question for this day's uproar, there being no cause whereby we may give an account of this concourse. 41 And when he had thus spoken, he dismissed the assembly.

EXPOSITION

Let us take up the story again from verse 20. It is tolerably certain that between verses 20 and 31, Paul wrote 1 *Corinthians,* in A.D. 57 (but this is his second letter to Corinth, 1 Cor. v. 9, 11). Read again Acts xviii. 1–17 ; then, 1 Corinthians. Verses 21, 22, are wonderful, revealing as they do Paul's solicitude for his converts, and his noble contempt for idleness. What dreams he dreams ! MACEDONIA, ACHAIA, JERUSALEM, ROME ! Truly neither Alexander, nor Caesar nor any hero of antiquity was a match for this little Benjamite in the magnanimity of his designs. What follows is illustrative of the age-long conflict between truth and error, right and wrong, holiness and sin, Christ and the devil ; for that's what it amounts to. Though what Demetrius says is exaggerated, he bears, unwittingly, a magnificent testimony to the power of the Gospel, and the work of Paul (26).

Here is the first conference of a Trade Union (24, 25). A " vested interest " was being attacked, and it squealed, as all such interests do, liquor, gambling, impurity. Christianity need not directly attack these to rouse them to hot hostility ; it has only to proclaim itself, and that is the most powerful condemnation of all that is opposed to it. Of course, we should also attack directly. We see here how selfishness in private (25) can turn to piety in public (27). Here also, is an illustration of crowd psychology (32–34). There are no riots so dangerous as religious riots, nor so fanatical.

Now listen to the Town Clerk, a very able man. He safeguards Gaius, Aristarchus, and Alexander, defends Paul against the charge made (37), rebukes Demetrius (38), and warns the crowd (36–40), while upholding the City's paganism (35, 36). His speech is a model of diplomacy.

And it should be noted that three things characterized the Christians at this time : *Faithfulness* to Christ and the Gospel ; *Courage,* both physical and moral (30–33) ; and *Prudence* (30, 31). We should relate and cultivate all virtues, and not develop one at the expense of another. Don't lose your head in a crowd.

Thought : HOW IMPOTENT IS GODLESS WRATH.

141

Title : AN INTERRUPTED SERMON

1 And after the uproar was ceased, Paul called unto him the disciples, and embraced them, and departed for to go into Macedonia. 2 And when he had gone over those parts, and had given them much exhortation, he came into Greece, 3 And there abode three months. And when the Jews laid wait for him, as he was about to sail into Syria, he purposed to return through Macedonia. 4 And there accompanied him into Asia Sopater of Berea ; and of the Thessalonians, Aristarchus and Secundus ; and Gaius of Derbe, and Timotheus ; and of Asia, Tychicus and Trophimus. 5 These going before tarried for us at Troas. 6 And we sailed away from Philippi after the days of unleavened bread, and came unto them to Troas in five days : where we abode seven days.

7 And upon the first day of the week, when the disciples came together to break bread, Paul preached unto them, ready to depart on the morrow ; and continued his speech until midnight. 8 And there were many lights in the upper chamber, where they were gathered together. 9 And there sat in a window a certain young man named Eutychus, being fallen into a deep sleep : and as Paul was long preaching, he sunk down with sleep, and fell down from the third loft, and was taken up dead. 10 And Paul went down, and fell on him, and embracing him said, Trouble not yourselves ; for his life is in him. 11 When he therefore was come up again, and had broken bread, and eaten, and talked a long while, even till break of day, so he departed. 12 And they brought the young man alive, and were not a little comforted.

EXPOSITION

" *After the uproar* "—what ? Will Paul take a month's holiday to recover from his nerve shock ? Not at all. He does not know the secret of masterly inactivity. Away he goes over his Macedonian field (1), which just means that he visited again Philippi, Thessalonica, and Berea, exhorting and encouraging the saints. On this journey, and in view of his intention to go into Greece, he wrote " 2 Corinthians," which read here. Then he went to Corinth (2), his third visit to that city, and there he abode *three months*; during which time he wrote " Galatians " and " Romans "; which read here.

The year is now A.D. 58. Being diverted from his original purpose, he went back through Macedonia, and crossed the sea from Neapolis to Troas (3, 6). Nine trusted friends were with him at this time, the seven of verse 4, and Silas and Luke. Sweet is companionship in days of storm and strain; and blessed is it to be kept at full stretch for Jesus Christ. The ten remained at Troas for a week (6). What memories this place would stir! (xvi. 8, 9).

What a Communion Service they had that Sunday evening, and Paul for the preacher! (7). He might well have rested that night, for in the morning he was to start out on a long journey; but no—he talked " *till break of day* " (7, 11). Very wrong inferences may be made from this incident. It is not a solemn warning to worshippers not to sleep in church, though, of course, they should not do so. Neither is it a rebuke to preachers who preach long sermons, though, of course, a sermon can be too long, as well as too short. The person who, falling asleep, fell and was killed, was a child, too young to appreciate Paul; but gladly did all the others sit up all night to listen to such a speaker. What preachers there were in bygone days! Yes, and what hearers! Eutychus was raised to life; and the party caught their boat (10, 11).

Thought: *LEAVE A FRAGRANT TRACK BE-HIND YOU.*

Title : *PAUL AND THE EPHESIAN ELDERS*

13 And we went before to ship, and sailed unto Assos, there intending to take in Paul : for so had he appointed, minding himself to go afoot. 14 And when he met with us at Assos, we took him in, and came to Mitylene. 15 And we sailed thence, and came the next day over against Chios ; and the next day we arrived at Samos, and tarried at Trogyllium ; and the next day we came to Miletus. 16 For Paul had determined to sail by Ephesus, because he would not spend the time in Asia : for he hasted, if it were possible for him, to be at Jerusalem the day of Pentecost. 17 And from Miletus he sent to Ephesus, and called the elders of the church. 18 And when they were come to him, he said unto them,

Ye know, from the first day that I came into Asia, after what manner I have been with you at all seasons, 19 Serving the Lord with all humility of mind, and with many tears, and temptations, which befell me by the lying in wait of the Jews : 20 And how I kept back nothing that was profitable unto you, but have shewed you, and have taught you publickly, and from house to house, 21 Testifying both to the Jews, and also to the Greeks, repentance toward God, and faith toward our Lord Jesus Christ. 22 And now, behold, I go bound in the spirit unto Jerusalem, not knowing the things that shall befall me there : 23 Save that the Holy Ghost witnesseth in every city, saying that bonds and afflictions abide me. 24 But none of these things move me, neither count I my life dear unto myself, so that I might finish my course with joy, and the ministry, which I have received of the Lord Jesus, to testify the gospel of the grace of God.

EXPOSITION

From Troas to Assos is about twenty miles. Paul tramped it, no doubt because he wanted time alone with God which he could not secure while his companions were with him (13). Do you ever feel that you *must* get away from nearest and dearest, on to the water, into the valley, up on the mountain, out in the country, anywhere, so long as you can be alone with God ; do you ? Paul got aboard at Assos, and sailed some two hundred miles to Miletus (14, 15). His reason for not going to Ephesus is given (16). " By " should be " *past* " (16, R.V.).

The Ephesian Elders met Paul at Miletus ; and a memorable meeting it was. What Paul said to them is recorded in verses 18–35. One point claims early attention (25, 38). This would appear to be a fear, and not a prophecy, for surely he did see their faces again (1 Tim. i. 3 ; iii. 14), unless room can be made for the Pastoral Epistles within the history of the "*Acts*" which is not likely.

Now consider this pathetic, yet heroic farewell address. Our life is divided into two parts, past and future ; the present is a mere point dividing the two. Paul looked *behind* with humble gratitude (18–21), and *before* with Christian courage (22–24). Pity the person that has no fruitful past, and no hopeful future. Paul's life was one of consecration (18, 19), fidelity (20, 27, 31), endurance (19), diligence and beneficence (33–35) ; and so he could anticipate suffering cheerfully (22, 23), for absorbed in his Master's service he was sublimely indifferent to his bodily estate (24). The two dominating notes of his message were *repentance* and *faith* (21), and where these are wanting there is no Gospel. The personal element is very prominent in this address as you will see from the occurrence of " *I*," " *me*," and " *my*." The occasion called for this, and the references are revealing. Note carefully the tenderness of Paul's farewell testimony (25–27), and the depth of the final exhortation (28–35). Let us all so live that we shall not be ashamed at last.

Thought : MARCH BREAST FORWARD, NEVER
DOUBTING CLOUDS WILL BREAK.

Title : *A PATHETIC FAREWELL*

25 And now, behold, I know that ye all, among whom I have gone preaching the kingdom of God, shall see my face no more. 26 Wherefore I take you to record this day, that I am pure from the blood of all men. 27 For I have not shunned to declare unto you all the counsel of God. 28 Take heed therefore unto yourselves, and to all the flock, over the which the Holy Ghost hath made you overseers, to feed the church of God, which he hath purchased with his own blood. 29 For I know this, that after my departing shall grievous wolves enter in among you, not sparing the flock. 30 Also of your own selves shall men arise, speaking perverse things, to draw away disciples after them. 31 Therefore watch, and remember, that by the space of three years I ceased not to warn every one night and day with tears. 32 And now, brethren, I commend you to God, and to the word of his grace, which is able to build you up, and to give you an inheritance among all them which are sanctified. 33 I have coveted no man's silver, or gold, or apparel. 34 Yea, ye yourselves know, that these hands have ministered unto my necessities, and to them that were with me. 35 I have shewed you all things, how that so labouring ye ought to support the weak, and to remember the words of the Lord Jesus, how he said, It is more blessed to give than to receive.

36 And when he had thus spoken, he kneeled down, and prayed with them all. 37 And they all wept sore, and fell on Paul's neck, and kissed him, 38 Sorrowing most of all for the words which he spake, that they should see his face no more. And they accompanied him unto the ship.

EXPOSITION

Look up EPHESUS on the map, " the commercial-metropolis of Asia. It stood between two chains of mountains, near the mouth of the loveliest ravine that cuts into the plateau of Asia Minor. From the city, roads radiated in every direction over the peninsular leading to the Aegean Sea, which gave it a surpassing position as a centre of trade. Its history is largely an account of the conflict between the enterprising Greek traders and the devotees of idolatrous worship and magical art." But what ultimately matters is that a Christian Church was there.

Read Acts xix. ; this farewell (17–28) ; the Epistle to the Ephesians ; and Revelation iii. 1–7 ; and remember that PAUL and JOHN both lived at Ephesus, the one to found the Church there, and the other to foster it. In all likelihood also, the mother of Jesus spent her later life there (John xix. 26, 27). These passages and particulars should profoundly impress us. Read Ramsay to know what Ephesus is like to-day.

What was the substance of Paul's ministry during his three years at Ephesus ? (20, 21, 25, 27, 35). *" The whole counsel of God "* means more now than it did then, because we have a fuller revelation. Let every preacher be faithful to what he knows of God, witnessing without fear or favour. The Church is a *flock*, blood-bought, and Spirit-fed (28). Perils and responsibilities are made plain in verses 28–31. The Church has ever been exposed to fierce foes and false friends, the latter being worse than the former (29, 30) ; our duty therefore is to *watch*, and *warn*, and *work* (31, 35).

Paul nobly illustrated a stray saying of Jesus' (33–35). Do you *really* believe that " it is *more* blessed to give than to receive " ? What a scene we have in verses 36–38 ! Listen to the supplication and the sobs : they were all *men*, remember. Paul dearly loved his converts and friends, and dearly did they love him. No doubt he was stern, but he must also have been tender and lovable. They watched the ship fade out of sight.

Thought : SAVE YOURSELF BY SELF-
FORGETFULNESS

Title : *THICK SHADOWS ON THE PATH*

1 And it came to pass, that after we were gotten from them, and had launched, we came with a straight course unto Coos, and the day following unto Rhodes, and from thence unto Patara : 2 And finding a ship sailing over unto Phenicia, we went aboard, and set forth. 3 Now when we had discovered Cyprus, we left it on the left hand, and sailed into Syria, and landed at Tyre : for there the ship was to unlade her burden. 4 And finding disciples, we tarried there seven days : who said to Paul through the Spirit, that he should not go up to Jerusalem. 5 And when we had accomplished those days, we departed and went our way ; and they all brought us on our way, with wives and children, till we were out of the city : and we kneeled down on the shore, and prayed. 6 And when we had taken our leave one of another, we took ship ; and they returned home again.

7 And when we had finished our course from Tyre, we came to Ptolemais, and saluted the brethren, and abode with them one day. 8 And the next day we that were of Paul's company departed, and came unto Cæsarea : and we entered into the house of Philip the evangelist, which was one of the seven ; and abode with him. 9 And the same man had four daughters, virgins, which did prophesy. 10 And as we tarried there many days, there came down from Judæa a certain prophet, named Agabus. 11 And when he was come unto us, he took Paul's girdle, and bound his own hands and feet, and said, Thus saith the Holy Ghost, So shall the Jews at Jerusalem bind the man that owneth this girdle, and shall deliver him into the hands of the Gentiles. 12 And when we heard these things, both we, and they of that place, besought him not to go up to Jerusalem. 13 Then Paul answered, What mean ye to weep and to break mine heart ? for I am ready not to be bound only, but also to die at Jerusalem for the name of the Lord Jesus. 14 And when he would not be persuaded, we ceased, saying, The will of the Lord be done.

EXPOSITION

With this passage concludes Paul's THIRD MIS-
SIONARY JOURNEY. Follow the track from Ephesus
(xix. 1), by M.G.M.T.A.M.C.S.M.C.R.P.T.P.C. to
Jerusalem. What about the journey from Assos to
Patara, and from there to Tyre ? What would these
men talk about ! I wonder if they were sea-sick !
They had our sea feelings in those days without our
sea comforts. These groups of disciples everywhere
(4, 7, 8) must have been to these hungry hearts what
food depots are to Arctic travellers. Wherever there
is a Christian, God has a foothold.

Luke kept a diary ; mark the minute details of
this record : a day here, seven there, an act, a
warning, women and children—all in the mosaic of
a Divine plan. As grains of sand make the shore,
and drops of water the ocean, so do hours and days,
words and deeds, tears and laughter, sorrow and
rapture, make up what we call *life*. Everything
counts. The outstanding lesson of our portion is
this : *each of us must do what God tells us to do*. God
told Paul to go to Jerusalem.

Now read verses 4, 10–14. One of the most difficult
problems of practical life is to know what are the
fixed points on which we must not give way, to which
all other considerations must yield, and what are the
points which may be yielded under the pressure of
conflicting circumstances. And never is the choice
of a course made so difficult as when the pleading of
our best friends is on the one side, and our convictions
are on the other. Luther said : " *Were there as many
devils in Worms as tiles on the roofs, I would go in.*"
And Paul said : " *I am ready to die for the name of the
Lord Jesus* " (13). Weeping may break a heart (13),
but it should not break a resolution formed in the
sight of God and by His Spirit. IF HE BIDS THEE—
RISE AND GO.

Thought : BE UNYIELDINGLY TRUE TO GOD
AND YOUR CONSCIENCE.

149

Title : CONFORMITY, OR NONCONFORMITY ?

15 And after those days we took up our carriages, and went up to Jerusalem. 16 There went with us also certain of the disciples of Cæsarea, and brought with them one Mnason of Cyprus, an old disciple, with whom we should lodge.

17 And when we were come to Jerusalem, the brethren received us gladly. 18 And the day following Paul went in with us unto James ; and all the elders were present. 19 And when he had saluted them, he declared particularly what things God had wrought among the Gentiles by his ministry. 20 And when they heard it, they glorified the Lord, and said unto him, Thou seest, brother, how many thousands of Jews there are which believe ; and they are all zealous of the law : 21 And they are informed of thee, that thou teachest all the Jews which are among the Gentiles to forsake Moses, saying that they ought not to circumcise their children, neither to walk after the customs. 22 What is it therefore ? the multitude must needs come together : for they will hear that thou art come. 23 Do therefore this that we say to thee : We have four men which have a vow on them ; 24 Them take, and purify thyself with them, and be at charges with them, that they may shave their heads : and all may know that those things, whereof they were informed concerning thee, are nothing ; but that thou thyself also walkest orderly, and keepest the law. 25 As touching the Gentiles which believe, we have written and concluded that they observe no such thing, save only that they keep themselves from things offered to idols, and from blood, and from strangled, and from fornication. 26 Then Paul took the men, and the next day purifying himself with them entered into the temple, to signify the accomplishment of the days of purification, until that an offering should be offered for every one of them.

EXPOSITION

Verses 15, 16, are both terminal and germinal : one great part of Paul's programme here ends, and another begins : on the one side are HIS TIRELESS ACTIVITIES, and on the other side are HIS FRUITFUL CAPTIVITIES. Here (16) a man is immortalized in eight words (Gr). Five things are said of him : 1. Mnason ; 2, of Cyprus ; 3, a disciple ; 4, early converted ; 5, entertained Paul and those who were with him.

AT JERUSALEM (xxi. 17 to xxiii. 22). What now follows is of profound importance, and in speaking of it, caution rather than dogmatism is needed. The situation is this : *Mosaism was setting ; Christianity was rising*, and transition periods are always difficult. What is to be done ? Are Gentile converts to be put under the Law ? or, are Jewish and Gentile Christians at once to enter into Christian liberty ? or are Jewish converts still to conform to the law, and Gentile converts be absolved ? The bigoted Jews were for the first ; Paul's party were for the second ; and James' party were for the third, which was a compromise of the other two. Now compromises are delicate, and may easily be dangerous things. If by a compromise, policy can be served without the sacrifice of principle, it is justifiable.

How often it happens that two parties, representing different streams of thought or practice, are unavoidably thrown together. What is to be done ? If both are unbending, something will be broken. But the question here is, " Did Paul do right to take that vow ? " (23, 24, 26). I would not dogmatize on that point ; but this may be said, that if his doing so was justifiable, it did not serve the purpose it was intended to : see what follows. This fact does not *prove* that he was wrong ; it may prove that some people are irreconcilable, do what one will. On the other hand, the advice of many should never be allowed to stampede any of us into a false position.

Thought : CHRIST CAN SOLVE YOUR PRE- SENT PROBLEM.

Title : A MERCIFUL DELIVERANCE

27 And when the seven days were almost ended,
the Jews which were of Asia, when they saw him in
the temple, stirred up all the people, and laid hands
on him, 28 Crying out, Men of Israel, help : This
is the man, that teacheth all men every where
against the people, and the law, and this place :
and further brought Greeks also into the temple,
and hath polluted this holy place. 29 (For they had
seen before with him in the city Trophimus an
Ephesian, whom they supposed that Paul had
brought into the temple.) 30 And all the city was
moved, and the people ran together : and they took
Paul, and drew him out of the temple : and forthwith the doors were shut.

31 And as they went about to kill him, tidings
came unto the chief captain of the band, that all
Jerusalem was in an uproar. 32 Who immediately
took soldiers and centurions, and ran down unto
them : and when they saw the chief captain and
the soldiers, they left beating of Paul. 33 Then
the chief captain came near, and took him, and
commanded him to be bound with two chains ;
and demanded who he was, and what he had done.
34 And some cried one thing, some another, among
the multitude : and when he could not know the
certainty for the tumult, he commanded him to be
carried into the castle. 35 And when he came
upon the stairs, so it was, that he was borne of the
soldiers for the violence of the people. 36 For the
multitude of the people followed after crying
Away with him.

37 And as Paul was to be led into the castle, he
said unto the chief captain, May I speak unto thee ?
Who said, Canst thou speak Greek ? 38 Art not thou
that Egyptian, which before these days madest an
uproar, and leddest out into the wilderness four
thousand men that were murderers ? 39 But Paul
said, I am a man which am a Jew of Tarsus, a city
in Cilicia, a citizen of no mean city : and I beseech
thee, suffer me to speak unto the people. 40 And
when he had given him licence, Paul stood on the

stairs, and beckoned with the hand unto the people. And when there was made a great silence, he spake unto them in the Hebrew tongue, saying,

EXPOSITION

Paul made a compromise to avoid a conflict, but he did not succeed. Suppose he had declined the advice of the Elders (18–25), the result could not have been worse than it now is, and it might have been better. Of course, it is easy to be wise after the event, but the whole affair calls our attention to *the desirability of compromise sometimes, and the peril of it at all times.*

The result of Paul's action is that he was a prisoner for the next five years, A.D. 58–63 : first at JERUSALEM (xxi. 17 to xxiii. 22) ; then, at CÆSAREA (xxiii. 23 to xxvi. 32) ; and finally, at ROME (xxvii to xxviii). But how amazingly fruitful were these captivities ! Truly, " *out of the eater came forth meat, and out of the strong, sweetness.*" Here two things are thrown into sharp contrast by being related : *fanaticism* and *fortitude* ; the Jews exhibiting the one, and Paul, the other. Two things, it should be observed, marked the fanaticism of these Jews : *lying* and *violence* ; and both are vices. Paul raised no opposition to the Law (28, cf. 26) ; neither had he defiled the Temple, for he had *not* taken Trophimus into it (28, 29). " *They supposed.*" Yes, supposition has broken countless hearts, ruined families, and shaken the foundations of nations. A supposition is never strong enough to build upon. Is your attitude towards somebody just now, based on a supposition ?

Why should Paul have been beaten before he was tried ? (32). Truth and right are never dependent on, and never resort to, such methods. Over against all this we see Paul calm, courageous, energetic, resourceful, courteous, sweetly reasonable. " *Away with him* " (36). That was said once before. Of whom ? " *The servant is not greater than his Lord.*"

This " chief captain " was a sensible man. What a pulpit (40), what a congregation (36), what a " platform " (35), and what a preacher! (40). Listen.

Thought : BE SURE TO KEEP YOUR MORAL BALANCE.

THE ACTS xxii. 1-16

Title : A NEW MAN

1 Men, brethren, and fathers, hear ye my defence which I make now unto you.

2 (And when they heard that he spake in the Hebrew tongue to them, they kept the more silence : and he saith,)

3 I am verily a man which am a Jew, born in Tarsus, a city in Cilicia, yet brought up in this city at the feet of Gamaliel, and taught according to the perfect manner of the law of the fathers, and was zealous toward God, as ye all are this day. 4 And I persecuted this way unto the death, binding and delivering into prisons both men and women. 5 As also the high priest doth bear me witness, and all the estate of the elders : from whom also I received letters unto the brethren, and went to Damascus, to bring them which were there bound unto Jerusalem, for to be punished.

6 And it came to pass, that, as I made my journey, and was come nigh unto Damascus about noon, suddenly there shone from heaven a great light round about me. 7 And I fell unto the ground, and heard a voice saying unto me, Saul, why persecutest thou me ? 8 And I answered, Who art thou, Lord ? And he said unto me, I am Jesus of Nazareth, whom thou persecutest. 9 And they that were with me saw indeed the light, and were afraid ; but they heard not the voice of him that spake to me. 10 And I said, What shall I do, Lord ? And the Lord said unto me, Arise, and go into Damascus ; and there

it shall be told thee of all things which are appointed for thee to do.

11 And when I could not see for the glory of that light, being led by the hand of them that were with me, I came into Damascus. 12 And one Ananias, a devout man according to the law, having a good report of all the Jews which dwelt there, 13 Came unto me, and stood, and said unto me, Brother Saul, receive thy sight. And the same hour I looked up upon him. 14 And he said, The God of our fathers hath chosen thee, that thou shouldest know his will, and see that Just One, and shouldest hear the voice of his mouth. 15 For thou shalt be his witness unto all men of what thou hast seen and heard. 16 And now why tarriest thou? arise, and be baptized, and wash away thy sins, calling on the name of the Lord.

EXPOSITION

Paul made his DEFENCE before four parties; (a) *The People* (ch. xxii.) ; (b) *The Council* (ch. xxiii.) ; (c) *The Roman Governors* (chs. xxiv.–xxvi.) ; before FELIX (24), FESTUS (25), and AGRIPPA (26) ; and finally, before (d) *Cæsar* (2 Tim. ii. 16). Don't imagine that this captivity period was lost time. Think of how, for nearly nineteen hundred years the Christian Church has been enriched thereby. Read on to verse 21. What an audience ! (xxi. 36), but when he spake to them in the Hebrew tongue, they listened (2). If we would command people's attention, we must speak to them in a language they can understand. The command was—" feed my lambs," not " feed my giraffes." The address falls into three parts in relation to Paul's conversion.

1. BEFORE CONVERSION (1–5). With consummate tact he makes contact with the audience in a way calculated to produce sympathy. He too was a Jew, had been taught by Gamaliel, knew the Law, had persecuted this new sect, had served the hand of the religious authorities. No preacher should begin by antagonising his audience.

2. AT CONVERSION (6–16). Here is the central part of Paul's defence. Verses 6–11 describe his vision of Jesus glorified, and 12–16 explain its significance. If no one could enter more perfectly into the feelings of his audience than he, so no one could have weightier reasons for changing his mind. He got converted, and he knew when and where. The change was not evolutionary, but cataclysmic.

How well he remembered it all, the Vision, the Voice, the darkness, the healing, the charge, the baptism. Have you had an experience of conversion ? The *actual* moment is not always the *conscious* moment ; but do you know at this moment that you are eternally saved ? What matters is the *experience*, not the *philosophy*. Christianity is a life before it is a doctrine.

Thought : GOD CAN TURN WOLVES INTO SHEEP

THE ACTS xxii. 17-30

Title : BOUND BUT NOT BEATEN

17 And it came to pass, that, when I was come again to Jerusalem, even while I prayed in the temple, I was in a trance ; 18 And saw him saying unto me, Make haste, and get thee quickly out of Jerusalem : for they will not receive thy testimony concerning me. 19 And I said, Lord, they know that I imprisoned and beat in every synagogue them that believed on thee : 20 And when the blood of thy martyr Stephen was shed, I also was standing by, and consenting unto his death, and kept the raiment of them that slew him. 21 And he said unto me, Depart : for I will send thee far hence unto the Gentiles.

22 And they gave him audience unto this word, and then lifted up their voices, and said, Away with such a fellow from the earth : for it is not fit that he should live. 23 And as they cried out, and cast off

their clothes, and threw dust into the air, **24 The chief captain commanded him to be brought into the castle, and bade that he should be examined by scourging ; that he might know wherefore they cried so against him. 25 And as they bound him with thongs, Paul said unto the centurion that stood by, Is it lawful for you to scourge a man that is a Roman, and uncondemned ? 26 When the centurion heard that, he went and told the chief captain, saying, Take heed what thou doest : for this man is a Roman. 27 Then the chief captain came, and said unto him, Tell me, art thou a Roman ? He said, Yea. 28 And the chief captain answered, With a great sum obtained I this freedom. And Paul said, But I was free born. 29 Then straightway they departed from him which should have examined him : and the chief captain also was afraid, after he knew that he was a Roman, and because he had bound him.**

30 On the morrow, because he would have known the certainty wherefore he was accused of the Jews, he loosed him from his bands, and commanded the chief priests and all their council to appear, and brought Paul down, and set him before them.

EXPOSITION

The third part of Paul's testimony relates to : 3. AFTER CONVERSION (17–21). Here Paul justifies his mission to the Gentiles, as, in 6–16, he had justified his faith in Jesus Christ. With verses 17–21, compare ch. ix. 28–30. It is a terrible thing when a soul or a city will not receive a preacher's testimony concerning Christ (18). What we want, and what God wills, do not always harmonise (18–21). When that is so, our *want* must give way to His *will*. In verses 1–21, Paul faced the Jews ; in 22–39, he faces the Romans. Mark how he relates himself to each. Is there anything more perilous than prejudice, or more foolish than fanaticism ? (22–23). The word " *Gentiles* " was like a match to gun powder : the magazine exploded. " *Not fit to live* " indeed ! (22). Then, who is ? Stand at a safe distance and watch that crowd

157

(23). What asylum could hold them all! Well, what next? Ignorance and violence generally go together (24). How cruel is power when divorced from righteousness. But earthly power has to reckon with Divine Providence (25, 26).

Paul was the only man of the first century of our era who united in himself all the qualities which could give a man access to the whole world. He was a HEBREW by birth, a GREEK by training, and a ROMAN by inheritance. Here he stood upon his Roman rights. He did not at Philippi (ch. xvi.). Why? We may be quite sure that now he had some good reason for his protests, and quite sure also that it was not a selfish one. He always considered first, not himself, but the interests of the Church and Kingdom of God. There are times when we are justified in claiming what is due to us as citizens.

Paul was *twice freeborn* (28). He had a Roman and a Heavenly citizenship. The latter cannot be acquired, as could the former, by wealth, merit, or effort, but only by regeneration. " *Ye must be born again.*" Are you? Read Philippians iii. 20, 21, R.V.

Thought : *THOUGHT HEAVEN IS THE GOAL,*

EARTH IS THE TRACK.

THE ACTS xxiii. 1-16

Title : *ETHICAL TANGLES*

1 And Paul, earnestly beholding the council, said, Men and brethren, I have lived in all good conscience before God until this day.

2 And the high priest Ananias commanded them that stood by him to smite him on the mouth. 3 Then said Paul unto him, God shall smite thee, thou whited wall: for sittest thou to judge me after the law, and commandest me to be smitten contrary

to the law ? 4 And they that stood by said, Revilest thou God's high priest ? 5 Then said Paul, I wist not, brethren, that he was the high priest : for it is written, Thou shalt not speak evil of the ruler of thy people.

6 But when Paul perceived that the one part were Sadducees, and the other Pharisees, he cried out in the council, Men and brethren, I am a Pharisee, the son of a Pharisee : of the hope and resurrection of the dead I am called in question. 7 And when he had so said, there arose a dissension between the Pharisees and the Sadducees : and the multitude was divided. 8 For the Sadducees say that there is no resurrection, neither angel, nor spirit : but the Pharisees confess both. 9 And there arose a great cry : and the scribes that were of the Pharisees' part arose, and strove, saying, We find no evil in this man : but if a spirit or an angel hath spoken to him, let us not fight against God. 10 And when there arose a great dissension, the chief captain, fearing lest Paul should have been pulled in pieces of them, commanded the soldiers to go down, and to take him by force from among them, and to bring him into the castle.

11 And the night following the Lord stood by him, and said, Be of good cheer, Paul : for as thou hast testified of me in Jerusalem, so must thou bear witness also at Rome.

12 And when it was day, certain of the Jews banded together, and bound themselves under a curse, saying that they would neither eat nor drink till they had killed Paul. 13 And they were more than forty which had made this conspiracy. 14 And they came to the chief priests and elders, and said, We have bound ourselves under a great curse, that we will eat nothing until we have slain Paul. 15 Now therefore ye with the council signify to the chief captain that he bring him down unto you to morrow, as though ye would enquire something more perfectly concerning him : and we, or ever he come near, are ready to kill him. 16 And when Paul's sister's son heard of their lying in wait, he went and entered into the castle, and told Paul.

EXPOSITION

In ch. xxii. 1–29, Paul makes his DEFENCE before the *people*. Here, in xxii. 30, to xxiii. 11, he makes it before the *Council*. Look now at verses 1–11. There are few passages which present so many difficulties in so small a space. Was it right for Paul to speak as he did in verse 3 ? How was it that he did not know that the High Priest was presiding ? If he was right in speaking as he did in verse 3, could he also be right in apologizing ? (5). Did he do right in classifying himself with the Pharisaic party, seeing that he was so far removed from them in spirit ? (6) ; and, in any case, was " *the hope and resurrection of the dead* " the count on which he had been arrested ? Was he justified in adopting a policy which had for its design the breaking of the impact of opposition against himself ? (7–9).

These questions are as fair as they are difficult. Think them out for yourself. I offer a few guiding remarks. 1. I will not say whether Paul spoke in *anger* or *indignation* in verse 3, but these should always be distinguished. We seldom do well to be angry ; we often do well to be indignant. Anger suggests feeling mastering judgment ; indignation suggests judgment giving character to feeling. 2. Several suppositions could clear up the second question (5a). Historically, this office at that time had fallen vacant, and Ananias, a deposed High Priest, was acting *pro tem*. But perhaps Paul was *short-sighted* (Gal. iv. 15). 3. Two replies may be given to the question of 5b : first, that it is possible to greatly respect an *office*, and yet have only contempt for the one who holds it ; second, that if one is convinced he has made a mistake, it is the right, manly, and Christian thing to say so. 4. The last three questions, as indeed them all, we must consider in the light of verse 11, " *Be of good cheer.*" Then the Lord was pleased with Paul ! This does not prove that Paul had acted wisely throughout, but it does show that his heart was right with God. But, for me, verse 5 remains a problem. What does ch. xxiv. 20, 21, mean ?

Thought : OUR BEST JUDGMENT IS NOT INFALLIBLE.

THE ACTS xxiii. 17-35

Title : A MIDNIGHT GALLOP

17 Then Paul called one of the centurions unto him, and said, Bring this young man unto the chief captain : for he hath a certain thing to tell him. 18 So he took him, and brought him to the chief captain, and said, Paul the prisoner called me unto him, and prayed me to bring this young man unto thee, who hath something to say unto thee. 19 Then the chief captain took him by the hand, and went with him aside privately, and asked him, What is that thou hast to tell me ? 20 And he said, The Jews have agreed to desire thee that thou wouldest bring down Paul to-morrow into the council, as though they would enquire somewhat of him more perfectly. 21 But do not thou yield unto them : for there lie in wait for him of them more than forty men, which have bound themselves with an oath, that they will neither eat nor drink till they have killed him : and now are they ready, looking for a promise from thee. 22 So the chief captain then let the young man depart, and charged him, See thou tell no man that thou hast shewed these things to me. 23 And he called unto him two centurions, saying, Make ready two hundred soldiers to go to Cæsarea, and horsemen threescore and ten, and spearmen two hundred, at the third hour of the night ; 24 And provide them beasts, that they may set Paul on, and bring him safe unto Felix the governor. 25 And he wrote a letter after this manner :

26 Claudius Lysias unto the most excellent governor Felix sendeth greeting. 27 This man was taken of the Jews, and should have been killed of them : then came I with an army, and rescued him, having understood that he was a Roman.

28 And when I would have known the cause wherefore they accused him, I brought him forth into their council : 29 Whom I perceived to be accused of questions of their law, but to have nothing laid to his charge worthy of death or of bonds. 30 And when it was told me how that the Jews laid wait for the man, I sent straightway to thee, and gave commandment to his accusers also to say before thee what they had against him. Farewell.

31 Then the soldiers, as it was commanded them, took Paul, and brought him by night to Antipatris. 32 On the morrow they left the horsemen to go with him, and returned to the castle : 33 Who, when they came to Cæsarea, and delivered the epistle to the governor, presented Paul also before him. 34 And when the governor had read the letter, he asked of what province he was. And when he understood that he was of Cilicia ; 35 I will hear thee, said he, when thine accusers are also come. And he commanded him to be kept in Herod's judgment hall.

EXPOSITION

In verses 11–22,, ends *the Jerusalem captivity*, and in 23–25, begins *the Cæsarean* captivity.

1. After two days of incessant strain Paul was much depressed. Physical and mental reactions are inevitable. This great man had them, so you need not wonder if you have. *But light came in the night.* The Lord's words met Paul's need as key fits lock (11). " *Cheer up Paul. Your Jerusalem witness has not been a failure ; and your work is not done yet.*" If the Master praises, we need not trouble ourselves about men.

God fulfils His purposes and promises in many ways ; sometimes by *miracle*, but more often by *providence*. Here are more than forty men who are resolved to kill Paul (13). The Lord, on the other hand, says that he shall see Rome (11). The odds are all against the forty. What became of these ? (12). Did they keep their vow ? Paul had a sister, and she had a son, and God used the lad in bringing deliverance to his servant. The nephew played his part well (16–22). We cannot all be engines, but we can be nuts and screws in the moral machinery of the world. Let no one imagine that his honest effort will not count. It will, and does.

2. Study carefully CLAUDIA LYSIAS, from xxi. 31 to xxiii. 30. The missionary prisoner travels like a king. Look at him, with a body-guard of four hundred and seventy soldiers, and riding, not walking ! (23, 24). What a scene ! Off to Cæsarea, sixty-eight Roman miles from Jerusalem. Here is the second *Letter* in the " Acts " record (26–30 : cf. xv. 23–29). Did Lysias speak the truth in verse 27 ? Paul arrives at Cæsarea, after fifteen hours in the saddle. He has seen Jerusalem *for the last time* ! It is now A.D. 59. The shuttles fly to and fro ; the dark and silver threads are interweaving ; the tangled skein is working out on the upper side a perfect pattern. Why not leave the tapestry of your life in the hands of the Divine Weaver ? He knows how to mend broken threads.

Thought : IN ALL OUR CHANGES WE HAVE
  THE CHANGELESS CHRIST.

THE ACTS xxiv. 1-9

Title : *A HIRED ORATOR*

1 And after five days Ananias the high priest descended with the elders, and with a certain orator named Tertullus, who informed the governor against Paul. 2 And when he was called forth, Tertullus began to accuse him, saying,

Seeing that by thee we enjoy great quietness, and that very worthy deeds are done unto this nation by thy providence, 3 We accept it always, and in all places, most noble Felix, with all thankfulness. 4 Notwithstanding, that I be not further tedious unto

thee, I pray thee that thou wouldest hear us of thy clemency a few words. 5 For we have found this man a pestilent fellow, and a mover of sedition among all the Jews throughout the world, and a ringleader of the sect of the Nazarenes : 6 Who also hath gone about to profane the temple : whom we took, and would have judged according to our law. 7 But the chief captain Lysias came upon us, and with great violence took him away out of our hands, 8 Commanding his accusers to come unto thee : by examining of whom thyself mayest take knowledge of all these things, whereof we accuse him. 9 And the Jews also assented, saying that these things were so.

EXPOSITION

Relative to Paul, we have in this chapter the *Indictment* (1-9), the *Defence* (10-21), and the *Result* (22-27). Construct the scene, and behold the characters. Felix, Paul, Ananias, Tertullus, Romans, Jews. What a conjunction of morality and immorality, of justice and injustice, of godliness and paganism !

Look, first of all, at 1. THE INDICTMENT (1-9). The Jews hired a professional orator to arraign a fellow Jew before a Roman governor. To what base depth will malice not stoop ! The address of Tertullus is in verses 2-8, and it is characterized by two things, *flattery*, and *falsehood*. (i) FLATTERY (2-4). This is a very dangerous thing, injuring both the flatterer and the flattered. Sir Walter Raleigh said that " *flatterers are the worst kind of traitors.*" Mark what this man said about Felix. But what are the facts ? Tacitus, the Roman historian, says that Felix thought he could commit any crime with impunity, and speaks of him as a ruler of boundless cruelty and profligacy, using the power of a king with the temper of a slave. Within two years of this event he was recalled from his province, and accused by the Jews at Rome (27). Now read the speech of Tertullus again.

The second characteristic is:—(ii) FALSEHOOD
(5–6). Listen to the rasp in these words, "*pestilence,
sedition, ringleader, sect, the Nazarenes.*" Paul is
charged with political rebellion, heresy, sacrilege,
and disorder. A pack of lies! Poor indeed is that
cause which must be propped up by untruth. (The
major part of verses 6–8, is omitted by the R.V.)
All the Jews who *assented* were liars also (9). To
nod to a lie is to tell one. There come times when
silence is immoral, when not to protest is to connive
at evil. These Jews were guilty of that.

Thought : WORDS ARE MORAL MONEY,
WHERE ARE YOURS MINTED?

THE ACTS xxiv. 10-27

Title : FELIX THE FOOLISH

**10 Then Paul, after that the governor had
beckoned unto him to speak, answered,**

**Forasmuch as I know that thou hast been of many
years a judge unto this nation, I do the more cheerfully answer for myself : 11 Because that thou
mayest understand, that there are yet but twelve
days since I went up to Jerusalem for to worship.
12 And they neither found me in the temple disputing with any man, neither raising up the people,
neither in the synagogues, nor in the city :
13 Neither can they prove the things whereof they
now accuse me. 14 But this I confess unto thee,
that after the way which they call heresy, so worship
I the God of my fathers, believing all things which
are written in the law and in the prophets : 15 And
have hope toward God, which they themselves also
allow, that there shall be a resurrection of the dead,
both of the just and unjust. 16 And herein do
I exercise myself, to have always a conscience void
of offence toward God, and toward men. 17 Now
after many years I came to bring alms to my nation,
and offerings. 18 Whereupon certain Jews from
Asia found me purified in the temple, neither with**

multitude, nor with tumult. 19 Who ought to have been here before thee, and object, if they had ought against me. 20 Or else let these same here say, if they have found any evil doing in me, while I stood before the council, 21 Except it be for this one voice, that I cried standing among them, Touching the resurrection of the dead I am called in question by you this day.

22 And when Felix heard these things, having more perfect knowledge of that way, he deferred them, and said, When Lysias the chief captain shall come down, I will know the uttermost of your matter. 23 And he commanded a centurion to keep Paul, and to let him have liberty, and that he should forbid none of his acquaintance to minister or come unto him. 24 And after certain days, when Felix came with his wife Drusilla, which was a Jewess, he sent for Paul, and heard him concerning the faith in Christ. 25 And as he reasoned of righteousness, temperance, and judgment to come, Felix trembled, and answered, Go thy way for this time ; when I have a convenient season, I will call for thee. 26 He hoped also that money should have been given him of Paul, that he might loose him : wherefore he sent for him the oftener, and communed with him. 27 But after two years Porcius Festus came into Felix' room : and Felix, willing to shew the Jews a pleasure, left Paul bound.

EXPOSITION

Now consider—2. THE DEFENCE (10–21). What a contrast to the previous speech ! Paul's reply is courteous, dignified, calm, frank, fearless, challenging, and conciliatory. It is both negative and positive : here we have a clear and bold denial, and a candid statement of facts. There is courtesy, but not flattery ; truth, and not falsehood ; fairness, and not malice ; respect, and not contempt ; argument, but not abuse, and, let us remember, abuse is never argument. Paul's defence is convincing because of its correctness, cogency, and calmness. The negative part of the defence is in 11–13 ; and the positive, in

14-21. Read verses 5 and 12 together. How could all that crime be committed in less than a fortnight, during the major part of which time Paul was under arrest ? That lie gave itself away. Falsehood lacks the cement of consistency.

But after denial, is testimony (14-16). What these Jews called " *a sect* " (14, R.V.) was really " *The Way* " (14), with its beginning away back in the call of Abraham, and its end far on in resurrection and judgment (14, 15). Study verse 16, which describes *practical religion*. What is conscience ? what its sphere ? and what its limitation ? The natural conscience is not infallible, but when enlightened and enlivened by the Spirit of God, it should be heard and heeded.

3. THE RESULT (22-27). What pathetic reading is this ! How terrible to know what is right, and yet, not to do it ; to tremble at the truth, and yet, not to trust it (25). Felix was apparently free, but really bound. Paul was apparently bound, but really free. Think of the bound talking of giving liberty to the free ! (23, 26, 27). It is better to be physically bound and morally free, than physically free and morally bound. What heroic courage Paul displayed on this occasion ! (25). Are *you* waiting for a " *convenient season* " ? It will never come. Now is God's time, and yours. There is a " *judgment to come* " (25).

Thought : GUARD AGAINST MORAL AND SPIRITUAL ANÆMIA.

THE ACTS xxv. 1-12

Title : PERSISTENT TREACHERY AND RIGHTEOUS TENACITY

1 Now when Festus was come into the province, after three days he ascended from Cæsarea to Jerusalem. 2 Then the high priest and the chief

of the Jews informed him against Paul, and besought him, 3 And desired favour against him, that he would send for him to Jerusalem, laying wait in the way to kill him. 4 But Festus answered, that Paul should be kept at Cæsarea, and that he himself would depart shortly thither. 5 Let them therefore, said he, which among you are able, go down with me, and accuse this man, if there be any wickedness in him.

6 And when he had tarried among them more than ten days, he went down unto Cæsarea ; and the next day sitting on the judgment seat commanded Paul to be brought. 7 And when he was come, the Jews which came down from Jerusalem stood round about, and laid many and grievous complaints against Paul, which they could not prove. 8 While he answered for himself, Neither against the law of the Jews, neither against the temple, nor yet against Cæsar, have I offended any thing at all. 9 But Festus, willing to do the Jews a pleasure, answered Paul, and said, Wilt thou go up to Jerusalem, and there be judged of these things before me ? 10 Then said Paul, I stand at Cæsar's judgment seat, where I ought to be judged : to the Jews have I done no wrong, as thou very well knowest. 11 For if I be an offender, or have committed any thing worthy of death, I refuse not to die : but if there be none of these things whereof these accuse me, no man may deliver me unto them. I appeal unto Cæsar. 12 Then Festus, when he had conferred with the council, answered, Hast thou appealed unto Cæsar ? unto Cæsar shalt thou go.

EXPOSITION

Felix left Paul to Festus. With these examples before us, respect for Roman justice is impossible (xxiv. 27 ; and xxv. 9). Mark the persistent hatred of the Jews. Nothing could alter or mollify their venom. From the time of Paul's conversion to this hour they worried him from place to place. This is an Oriental, not an Occidental trait. The Jews requested that Paul be brought to Jerusalem. Why ? See verse 3, with xxiii. 12. No doubt these men were getting hungry. Suppose Festus had done as they desired ! We would never have had *Ephesians, Philippians, Colossians, Philemon,* and the *Pastoral Epistles !* Divine sovereignty controls human spite. God had said to Paul, " *thou must bear witness also at Rome* " (xxiii. 11). How unlikely that seemed at the time ; but now the way to the Capital is cut clean through Jewish injustice and Roman indecision. There may happen in a moment what has not happened in a millennium. There is no such thing as a *cul-de-sac* in the Christian's path.

What these Jews lacked in integrity they made up for in imagination (7, cf. xxiv. 13) ; they were as fertile as they were false. In the main, so we judge from Paul's answer (8), their charges against him were of *heresy, sacrilege,* and *treason.* To each he gave a categorical denial. How great a thing it is to have a clear conscience and a clean heart. Paul's appeal to Cæsar must have come as a great surprise to his friends, to the Jews, and to Festus ; nor could he himself have understood all that it would mean : yet, undoubtedly he was guided by God. There are times when we have to make up our minds quickly on some momentous issue, and then, much depends upon the state of our spiritual health. One who *lives* in the fellowship of God can sense much more quickly His will in a crisis than one who lives at a distance.

Thought : THE LONGEST WAY ROUND MAY
BE THE SAFEST WAY HOME.

THE ACTS xxv. 13-27

Title : CIVIL COURTESIES LEAD TO A COURT

13 And after certain days king Agrippa and Bernice came unto Cæsarea to salute Festus. 14 And when they had been there many days, Festus declared Paul's cause unto the king, saying, There is a certain man left in bonds by Felix : 15 About whom, when

I was at Jerusalem, the chief priests and the elders of the Jews informed me, desiring to have judgment against him. 16 To whom I answered, It is not the manner of the Romans to deliver any man to die, before that he which is accused have the accusers face to face, and have licence to answer for himself concerning the crime laid against him. 17 Therefore, when they were come hither, without any delay on the morrow I sat on the judgment seat, and commanded the man to be brought forth. 18 Against whom when the accusers stood up, they brought none accusation of such things as I supposed : 19 But had certain questions against him of their own superstition, and of one Jesus, which was dead, whom Paul affirmed to be alive. 20 And because I doubted of such manner of questions, I asked him whether he would go to Jerusalem, and there be judged of these matters. 21 But when Paul had appealed to be reserved unto the hearing of Augustus, I commanded him to be kept till I might send him to Cæsar. 22 Then Agrippa said unto Festus, I would also hear the man myself. To morrow, said he, thou shalt hear him.

23 And on the morrow, when Agrippa was come, and Bernice, with great pomp, and was entered into the place of hearing, with the chief captains, and principal men of the city, at Festus' commandmnet Paul was brought forth. 24 And Festus said, King Agrippa, and all men which are here present with us, ye see this man, about whom all the multitude of the Jews have dealt with me, both at Jerusalem, and also here, crying that he ought not to live any longer. 25 But when I found that he had committed nothing worthy of death, and that he himself hath appealed to Augustus, I have determined to send him. 26 Of whom I have no certain thing to write unto my lord. Wherefore I have brought him forth before you, and specially before thee, O king Agrippa, that, after examination had, I might have somewhat to write. 27 For it seemeth to me unreasonable to send a prisoner, and not withal to signify the crimes laid against him.

EXPOSITION

AGRIPPA of this narrative is HEROD AGRIPPA II. the son of HEROD AGRIPPA I. of Chapter xii, and the brother of the wife of FELIX, DRUSILLA (xxiv. 24). BERNICE is AGRIPPA'S sister (13). This scene in the audience-chamber of the governor at Cæsarea is indeed a strange one. Gerok says it may be viewed in three ways : 1. IT WAS A DRAWING-ROOM OF WORLDLY GLORY, by reason of the splendour of the assembled nobility. 2. IT WAS A LECTURE-ROOM OF HOLY DOCTRINE, by reason of the testimony of the Apostle Paul. 3. IT WAS A JUDGMENT-HALL OF DIVINE MAJESTY, by reason of the impression produced by the apostolic discourse.

Five things are here noticeable : *justice, ignorance, contempt, curiosity,* and *display.* (a) A sense of fair-play is reflected in verses 13–17. Festus here enunciates an elemental principle of justice, namely, that one accused should have an opportunity to defend himself (16) ; yet in social and church life are we not constantly forming estimates of people, on report, without any attempt to learn the truth ? Stop that ! (b) Festus owns up to his ignorance of the matters under dispute (20 R.V.). He says he was perplexed, and that was due to his ignorance. Roman governors were not conversant with Jewish theology. (c) But with Festus' ignorance went contempt (19) "*of one Jesus.*" ! Yet, that man was his Creator and Redeemer. Contempt of people is not a thing to cultivate. Contemptuous people are only exhibiting moral defect in themselves. (d) Curiosity may be good or bad (22). If it leads, as in the case of Zacchaeus, to concern and conversion, it is good ; but not so in the case before us. (e) "*Great pomp*" (23). Soon it was only dust, but the prisoner's word remains. "All flesh is as grass, and all the glory of man as the flower of grass." What a ridiculous thing is proud dust ; but how great a thing is Christian devotion and courage !

Thought : *THE CHRISTLESS CANNOT UNDER-STAND THE CHRISTIAN.*

Title : *THE INVINCIBILITY OF CHRISTIAN CERTITUDE*

1 Then Agrippa said unto Paul, Thou art permitted to speak for thyself. Then Paul stretched forth the hand, and answered for himself :

2 I think myself happy, king Agrippa, because I shall answer for myself this day before thee touching all the things whereof I am accused of the Jews : 3 Especially because I know thee to be expert in all customs and questions which are among the Jews : wherefore I beseech thee to hear me patiently. 4 My manner of life from my youth, which was at the first among mine own nation at Jerusalem, know all the Jews ; 5 Which knew me from the beginning, if they would testify, that after the most straitest sect of our religion I lived a Pharisee. 6 And now I stand and am judged for the hope of the promise made of God unto our fathers : 7 Unto which promise our twelve tribes, instantly serving God day and night, hope to come. For which hope's sake, king Agrippa, I am accused of the Jews. 8 Why should it be thought a thing incredible with you, that God should raise the dead ? 9 I verily thought with myself, that I ought to do many things contrary to the name of Jesus of Nazareth. 10 Which thing I also did in Jerusalem : and many of the saints did I shut up in prison, having received authority from the chief priests ; and when they were put to death, I gave my voice against them. 11 And I punished them oft in every synagogue, and compelled them to blaspheme ; and being exceedingly mad against them, I persecuted them even unto strange cities. 12 Whereupon as I went to Damascus with authority and commission from the chief priests, 13 At midday, O king, I saw in the way a light from heaven, above the brightness of the sun, shining round about me and them which journeyed with me. 14 And when we were all fallen to the earth, I heard a voice speaking unto me, and saying in the Hebrew tongue, Saul, Saul, why persecutest thou me ? it is hard for thee to kick against the pricks. 15 And I said, Who art thou, Lord ? And he said, I am Jesus whom thou per-

secutest. 16 But rise, and stand upon thy feet : for I have appeared unto thee for this purpose, to make thee a minister and a witness both of these things which thou hast seen, and of those things in the which I will appear unto thee ; 17 Delivering thee from the people, and from the Gentiles, unto whom now I send thee, 18 To open their eyes, and to turn them from darkness to light, and from the power of Satan unto God, that they may receive forgiveness of sins, and inheritance among them which are sanctified by faith that is in me.

EXPOSITION

This is the record of a notable event and a noble effort, and it is full of dramatic thrill : emotions are stirred as is the surface of a lake over which cross-current winds are running. Here is PAUL, still calm and dignified and eloquent ; and FESTUS, still contemptuous ; and AGRIPPA challenged and stricken of conscience ; and BERNICE, no doubt obdurate ; and I wonder what " *the chief captains and principal men of the city* " thought ! (xxv. 23). This is Paul's eighth speech, and the third account of his conversion. What a Christian gentleman he was, dignified, gentle, courteous ! And how conclusive was his testimony, based as it always was on facts. It is as though he said, " let the psychologists say what they please, I was a wolf, and am now a sheep, and the change came suddenly." In verses 2–23, 25–27, 29, is Paul's *defence*, and in verses 24, 28, 30–32, is the *effect* of it upon Festus, Agrippa, and the company. Observe the courteous opening (2, 3), the reference to *his life before conversion* (4–11), *his experience of conversion* (12–18), and *his witness after conversion* (19–23).

Numerous are the lessons which this speech would teach us. Note a few of them. A RESURRECTION OF THE BODY IS NOT INCREDIBLE (8). We must yield to facts, and the fact that Christ rose from the dead is unchallengeable.

CONSCIENCE IS NOT INFALLIBLE (9). We may be

sincere, without being *right*. IT IS BOTH DIFFICULT AND PERILOUS TO RESIST GOD (14). The figure is of oxen kicking the master's goad : it is fruitless resistance to a superior power. The proverb is classical, and found in many writers.

JESUS IS IN HEAVEN (15), the man of Nazareth ; and one day we shall *see* Him.

Verses 16 and 18 are very full. When Christ appears to us, it is *for a purpose* (16). There is more to be known than we yet know (16). Mark in verse 18, *conversion, illumination, emancipation*, and *sanctification*.

Thought : *HAVE YOU EVER TOLD HOW YOU WERE CONVERTED ?*

THE ACTS xxvi. 19-32

Title : *A PRISONER TALKS PLAINLY TO POTENTATES*

19 Whereupon, O king Agrippa, I was not disobedient unto the heavenly vision : 20 But shewed first unto them of Damascus, and at Jerusalem, and throughout all the coasts of Judæa, and then to the Gentiles, that they should repent and turn to God, and do works meet for repentance. 21 For these causes the Jews caught me in the temple, and went about to kill me. 22 Having therefore obtained help of God, I continued unto this day, witnessing both to small and great, saying none other things than those which the prophets and Moses did say should come : 23 That Christ should suffer, and that he should be the first that should rise from the dead, and should shew light unto the people, and to the Gentiles.

24 And as he thus spake for himself, Festus said with a loud voice, Paul, thou art beside thyself ; much learning doth make thee mad. 25 But he said, I am not mad, most noble Festus ; but speak forth the words of truth and soberness. 26 For the king knoweth of these things, before whom also I speak freely : for I am persuaded that none of these

things are hidden from him ; for this thing was not done in a corner. 27 King Agrippa, believest thou the prophets ? I know that thou believest. 28 Then Agrippa said unto Paul, Almost thou persuadest me to be a Christian. 29 And Paul said, I would to God, that not only thou, but also all that hear me this day, were both almost, and altogether such as I am, except these bonds.

30 And when he had thus spoken, the king rose up, and the governor, and Bernice, and they that sat with them : 31 And when they were gone aside, they talked between themselves, saying, This man doeth nothing worthy of death or of bonds. 32 Then said Agrippa unto Festus, This man might have been set at liberty, if he had not appealed unto Cæsar.

EXPOSITION

Let us look, first of all, at what remains of Paul's address, and then, at the effect it had on those present. Youth is the time for *vision* (19), and remember, Paul was a young man at the time of his conversion. All visions are not *heavenly*, but all heavenly visions should be *immediately obeyed*. You will not get another vision of God until you obey the last one you received. The true life is one of ever-widening usefulness (20) : " Damascus, Jerusalem, Judea, the Gentile world."

And observe these great notes of Paul's message : " *repent, turn, do*." No one can *do* until he *turns*, and no one will *turn* who does not *repent*. Don't try to begin at the end. He who will be faithful will be assailed (21). Is there anything more stupid than to suppose that truth is got rid of by killing the witness to it ? He whom God helps will continue (22). In God's sight none is *small*, and none is *great* : or, in another view, all are *small*, and all are *great*. In earth's view, some are small, and some are great, though, in reality many of the small are great, and many of the great are small. Spiritual enlightenment can come only by way of Christ's death and resurrection (23).

Now mark the effect of all this, first upon FESTUS (24), and then upon AGRIPPA (28). Each was affected in a different way, yet neither was won. Strange is it that it is only *Christian* enthusiasm that is put down to mental abnormality (24, Mark iii. 21). Both church and world need more madmen like Paul. Read Agrippa's utterance in the R.V. (27). Was the king sarcastic or sincere, do you suppose ? Anyhow, is it with you *almost,* or *altogether* ? (29). One may graze the gates of heaven on the way to hell.

> " *'Almost,'* can not avail,
> ' *Almost* ' is but to fail ;
> Sad, sad that bitter wail,
> ' *Almost* ' but lost.''

Look at verse 32. It was the king who was *bound,* and the prisoner who was *free.* Things are often not what they seem.

Thought : WE CANNOT PUT NOBILITY ON AND OFF WITH OUR CLOTHES.

THE ACTS xxvii. 1-17

Title : ALL ABOARD FOR ROME

1 And when it was determined that we should sail into Italy, they delivered Paul and certain other prisoners unto one named Julius, a centurion of Augustus' band. 2 And entering into a ship of Adramyttium, we launched, meaning to sail by the coasts of Asia ; one Aristarchus, a Macedonian of Thessalonica, being with us. 3 And the next day we touched at Sidon. And Julius courteously entreated Paul, and gave him liberty to go unto his friends to refresh himself. 4 And when we had launched from thence, we sailed under Cyprus, because the winds were contrary. 5 And when we had sailed over the sea of Cilicia and Pamphylia, we came to Myra, a city of Lycia. 6 And there the centurion found a ship of Alexandria sailing into

Italy; and he put us therein. 7 And when we had sailed slowly many days, and scarce were come over against Cnidus, the wind not suffering us, we sailed under Crete, over against Salmone; 8 And, hardly passing it, came unto a place which is called The Fair Havens; nigh whereunto was the city of Lasea.

9 Now when much time was spent, and when sailing was now dangerous, because the fast was now already past, Paul admonished them, 10 And said unto them, Sirs, I perceive that this voyage will be with hurt and much damage, not only of the lading and ship, but also of our lives. 11 Nevertheless the centurion believed the master and the owner of the ship, more than those things which were spoken by Paul. 12 And because the haven was not commodious to winter in, the more part advised to depart thence also, if by any means they might attain to Phenice, and there to winter; which is an haven of Crete, and lieth toward the south west and north west. 13 And when the south wind blew softly, supposing that they had obtained their purpose, loosing thence, they sailed close by Crete. 14 But not long after there arose against it a tempestuous wind, called Euroclydon. 15 And when the ship was caught, and could not bear up into the wind, we let her drive. 16 And running under a certain island which is called Clauda, we had much work to come by the boat: 17 Which when they had taken up, they used helps, undergirding the ship; and, fearing lest they should fall into the quicksands, strake sail, and so were driven.

EXPOSITION

The captivities at JERUSALEM and CÆSAREA are at an end, and the captivity at ROME begins (chs. xxvii, xxviii). These two chapters cover the years A.D. 60–63; and we see Paul, first, ON THE SEA (ch. xxvii), then, AT THE ISLAND (xxviii. 1–10), and finally, IN THE CITY (xxviii. 11–31). The "we" in verse 1 shows that Luke was one of the party. Connecting it with the "we" in xxi. 17, it seems clear that Luke was with Paul through the whole of these two eventful years, and that we owe this detailed narrative to this fact, as also almost certainly, Luke's Gospel, for which the two years at Cæsarea afforded an admirable opportunity.

The first thing to do on reading this chapter is to get a map of Paul's journeys, and carefully trace the route he took, and learn all you can about the places and circumstances. When that has been done we are free to see here a picture of LIFE'S JOURNEY. Bunyan wrote an immortal allegory of the Christian course as a journey *by land*. Here, we may see it as a journey *by sea*. What a variety there is of companionship! What a strange admixture of fellow-travellers, from whose company we cannot altogether disassociate ourselves! Like the *captain*, there are those who have a right to command us; like the *soldiers*, those in whose power we stand; like the *sailors*, those whose duty it is to care for our safety; like *Paul*, those who can enlighten us; like *Luke*, those who can heal us; like *Aristarchus*, those who can refresh us; and like the *prisoners*, those who are our fellow-sufferers.

The presence here of Romans, Macedonians, Alexandrians, Hebrews, and others, reminds us that this is a world of nations, and that we cannot stand clear of one another. On life's journey there can be no absolute seclusion, or refined retirement. And if there could, how would experience be gained, and where would be found the means of discipline and self-sacrifice ? "*No man liveth to himself.*" We are all on the ship and on the sea.

Thought : WE CANNOT ALWAYS CHOOSE OUR COMPANY.

THE ACTS xxvii. 18-29

Title : CHEER IN THE STORM

18 And we being exceedingly tossed with a tempest, the next day they lightened the ship ;
19 And the third day we cast out with our own hands

the tackling of the ship. 20 And when neither sun nor stars in many days appeared, and no small tempest lay on us, all hope that we should be saved was then taken away. 21 But after long abstinence Paul stood forth in the midst of them, and said, Sirs, ye should have hearkened unto me, and not have loosed from Crete, and to have gained this harm and loss. 22 And now I exhort you to be of good cheer : for there shall be no loss of any man's life among you, but of the ship. 23 For there stood by me this night the angel of God, whose I am, and whom I serve, 24 Saying, Fear not, Paul ; thou must be brought before Cæsar : and, lo, God hath given thee all them that sail with thee. 25 Wherefore, sirs, be of good cheer : for I believe God, that it shall be even as it was told me. 26 Howbeit we must be cast upon a certain island.

27 But when the fourteenth night was come, as we were driven up and down in Adria, about midnight the shipmen deemed that they drew near to some country ; 28 And sounded, and found it twenty fathoms : and when they had gone a little further, they sounded again, and found it fifteen fathoms. 29 Then fearing lest we should have fallen upon rocks, they cast four anchors out of the stern, and wished for the day.

EXPOSITION

Looking at this record as a picture of our journey over life's ocean, we have seen how varied is our company. But there are other points of analogy. On such a journey, difficulties, hardship, and peril are certainties ; the winds are sure to be contrary, and the sea may be tempestuous. Sometime or other sunshine will give place to storm. The changing drama of nature mirrors the story of the human soul. Life is not all radiant calm : we must expect also cyclonic disturbance. If sometimes our nights are turned into day by happy providences, sometimes our days are turned into night by that same Wisdom (20). What is it that avails at such times ? Only faith in God (23, 24).

Paul was the only hope of this ship, and though

a prisoner, he was really the ruler. The centurion and master of the ship may typify that blind obstinacy which will persevere with its designs in the teeth of nature's laws. But only the Christian religion can bring comfort and hope (24) in such circumstances as these. It is worthy of notice that, though no doubt Paul and his companions prayed, they also worked (19). God is in charge of the storm, but he will not handle "*the tackling of the ship*": we have to do that. With piety should go prudence, and with entreaty, effort. There is no use our telling men what they should not have done, unless we also can tell them what they now should do (21, 22). No matter what our circumstances may be, we should witness for Christ (23); "*whose I am, and whom I serve*," said Paul. You cannot serve Him unless you are His. Paul kept his head in this storm and God kept his heart. The world, like this ship, is greatly blessed because Christians are in it. Only Christian faith can be triumphant in the face of black despair.

Thought : LIFE IS NOT A PICNIC, BUT A PROBATION.

THE ACTS xxvii. 30-44

Title : A SCRAMBLE TO SHORE

30 And as the shipmen were about to flee out of the ship, when they had let down the boat into the sea, under colour as though they would have cast anchors out of the foreship, 31 Paul said to the centurion and to the soldiers, Except these abide in the ship, ye cannot be saved. 32 Then the soldiers cut off the ropes of the boat, and let her fall off. 33 And while the day was coming on, Paul besought them all to take meat, saying, This day is the fourteenth day that ye have tarried and continued fasting, having taken nothing. 34 Wherefore I pray you to take some meat : for this is for your health : for there shall not an hair fall from the head of any of you. 35 And when he had thus spoken, he took

bread, and gave thanks to God in presence of them all : and when he had broken it, he began to eat. 36 Then were they all of good cheer, and they also took some meat. 37 And we were in all in the ship two hundred threescore and sixteen souls. 38 And when they had eaten enough, they lightened the ship, and cast out the wheat into the sea. 39 And when it was day, they knew not the land : but they discovered a certain creek with a shore, into the which they were minded, if it were possible, to thrust in the ship. 40 And when they had taken up the anchors, they committed themselves unto the sea, and loosed the rudder bands, and hoisted up the mainsail to the wind, and made toward shore. 41 And falling into a place where two seas met, they ran the ship aground ; and the forepart stuck fast, and remained unmovable, but the hinder part was broken with the violence of the waves. 42 And the soldiers' counsel was to kill the prisoners, lest any of them should swim out, and escape. 43 But the centurion willing to save Paul, kept them from their purpose ; and commanded that they which could swim should cast themselves first into the sea, and get to land : 44 And the rest, some on boards, and some on broken pieces of the ship. And so it came to pass, that they escaped all safe to land.

EXPOSITION

What an amazing story this is. Think of these two hundred and seventy six souls not having eaten for a fortnight, during which time they were blown about and beaten by the reckless sea ! Then, see Paul among them, cheering them, and getting them to eat, serving them with food, and in presence of them all, aloud asking God's blessing on the bread (33-37). He must have been a good sailor. There's nothing like a storm at sea to shew what is in a man. The *shipmen*, whose duty it was to abide by the ship to the last, tried to escape (30). The *soldiers* thought the best thing to do was to kill the prisoners (42). The *Apostle* saved both situations : the one by his presence of mind (31), and the other, by his presence of body (43). The whole narrative is exceedingly graphic, and could have been given only by an eye witness, and one with nautical knowledge. The world may not like Christians, but it cannot get on without them.

Verse 41 tells of a wreck, and may well lead us to think of the *intellectual, moral,* and *spiritual* shipwreck which so many are making every day. Have you *run aground ?* Is your will stuck, and is your conscience broken ? (41). It is said of even Peter that he began to sink, but, happily for himself, he knew it, and cried to Christ for help. Alas for people who do not know it !

The closing verses (43, 44) tell of a landing. There are different ways of getting ashore—applying this to Christians : some with bold stroke swim in, and others miserably drift in on debris. How are you going home ?

Reverting to verse 32, let it be said that, but for the cutting of those ropes we would never have had *Ephesians, Philippians, Colossians,* or *Philemon* (31). Life's providences mysteriously and marvellously interlock, but the mind and hand behind them all are God's.

Thought : IF YOU CANNOT BE A GOOD LEADER, BE A GOOD FOLLOWER.

THE ACTS xxviii. 1-15

Title : AT MALTA AND TOWARDS ROME

1 And when they were escaped, then they knew that the island was called Melita. 2 And the barbarous people shewed us no little kindness : for they kindled a fire, and received us every one, because of the present rain, and because of the cold. 3 And when Paul had gathered a bundle of sticks, and laid them on the fire, there came a viper out of the heat, and fastened on his hand. 4 And when the barbarians saw the venomous beast hang on his hand, they said among themselves, No doubt this man is

a murderer, whom, though he hath escaped the sea, yet vengeance suffereth not to live. 5 And he shook off the beast into the fire, and felt no harm. 6 Howbeit they looked when he should have swollen, or fallen down dead suddenly : but after they had looked a great while, and saw no harm come to him, they changed their minds, and said that he was a god.

7 In the same quarters were possessions of the chief man of the island, whose name was Publius ; who received us, and lodged us three days courteously. 8 And it came to pass, that the father of Publius lay sick of a fever and of a bloody flux : to whom Paul entered in, and prayed, and laid his hands on him, and healed him. 9 So when this was done, others also, which had diseases in the island, came, and were healed : 10 Who also honoured us with many honours ; and when we departed, they laded us with such things as were necessary.

11 And after three months we departed in a ship of Alexandria, which had wintered in the isle, whose sign was Castor and Pollux. 12 And landing at Syracuse, we tarried there three days. 13 And from thence we fetched a compass, and came to Rhegium : and after one day the south wind blew, and we came the next day to Puteoli : 14 Where we found brethren, and were desired to tarry with them seven days : and so we went toward Rome. 15 And from thence, when the brethren heard of us, they came to meet us as far as Appii Forum, and The Three Taverns : whom when Paul saw, he thanked God, and took courage.

EXPOSITION.

Observe how carefully Luke kept his diary, notwithstanding the trying circumstances. The record is that of an eye witness, and the notes of *time* are given with exactness : " *three days* " (7) ; " *after three months* " (11) ; " *three days* " (12) ; " *after one day*," " *the second day* " (13) ; " *seven days* " (14). Mark also these particulars :—MALTA, PUBLIUS, THE TWIN BROTHERS, SYRACUSE, RHEGIUM, PUTEOLI, MARKET OF

Appius, The Three Taverns, Rome. Note also the references to *barbarians, rain, cold, sticks, viper, murdered, god, entertained, fever, dysentry, cured, honours.*

1. The Arrival at Malta (1-10). Paul and his company spent *three months* there, 276 of them, Christians and criminals, soldiers and sailors, Romans and Jews ! It is Paul who dominates the scene. The Church's greatest theologian gathers sticks for the fire. The heathen are hospitable, and show that *kindness* is universally a human quality. They also are superstitious (4), and unstable (6). It's a long stride from " *murderer* " to " *god,*" but these people easily took it. There is peril in the noblest service, and out of the fires of devotion vipers may fasten on us ; but *shake them off*, and get on with the work. Luke records the healing at Citta Vecchia, the old capital of the island, but Paul wrought it : it was the preacher, and not the physician who effected the cures. Medical missions are an essential part of the redeeming enterprise. I doubt not Paul left some Christians on this Island whom he did not find there when he landed.

2. From Malta to Rome (11-15). How sweet is friendship in Christ (14,15) ; how refreshing and encouraging. Paul, Luke and Aristarchus (27, 2) had a great *week* at Puteoli ! And their hearts kindled again when brethren came to meet them as they drew near to Rome. With a little thought we all could make life easier and happier for a lot of people.

Thought : CHRIST WOULD HAVE US FIT INTO OUR CIRCUMSTANCES.

THE ACTS xxviii. 16-31

Title : TWO YEARS' MINISTRY IN ROME

16 And when we came to Rome, the centurion delivered the prisoners to the captain of the guard :

but Paul was suffered to dwell by himself with a soldier that kept him.

17 And it came to pass, that after three days Paul called the chief of the Jews together : and when they were come together, he said unto them, Men and brethren, though I have committed nothing against the people, or customs of our fathers, yet was I delivered prisoner from Jerusalem into the hands of the Romans. 18 Who, when they had examined me, would have let me go, because there was no cause of death in me. 19 But when the Jews spake against it, I was constrained to appeal unto Cæsar ; not that I had ought to accuse my nation of. 20 For this cause therefore have I called for you, to see you, and to speak with you : because that for the hope of Israel I am bound with this chain. 21 And they said unto him, We neither received letters out of Judæa concerning thee, neither any of the brethren that came shewed or spake any harm of thee. 22 But we desire to hear of thee what thou thinkest : for as concerning this sect, we know that every where it is spoken against.

23 And when they had appointed him a day, there came many to him into his lodging ; to whom he expounded and testified the kingdom of God, persuading them concerning Jesus, both out of the law of Moses, and out of the prophets, from morning till evening. 24 And some believed the things which were spoken, and some believed not. 25 And when they agreed not among themselves, they departed, after that Paul had spoken one word, Well spake the Holy Ghost by Esaias the prophet unto our fathers, 26 Saying,

Go unto this people, and say, Hearing ye shall hear, and shall not understand ; and seeing ye shall see, and not perceive : 27 For the heart of this people is waxed gross, and their ears are dull of hearing, and their eyes have they closed ; lest they should see with their eyes, and hear with their ears, and understand with their heart, and should be converted, and I should heal them.

28 Be it known therefore unto you, that the salvation of God is sent unto the Gentiles, and that they will hear it. 29 And when he had said these

words, the Jews departed, and had great reasoning among themselves.

30 And Paul dwelt two whole years in his own hired house, and received all that came in unto him, 31 Preaching the kingdom of God, and teaching those things which concern the Lord Jesus Christ, with all confidence, no man forbidding him.

EXPOSITION

We have followed the Apostle ON THE SEA (ch. xxvii) and AT THE ISLAND (xxviii. 1-15) : and now we see him IN THE CITY (16-31). The following particulars should be carefully noted.

The company arrived at Rome in A.D. 61, and Paul remained there for two years. In A.D. 62, latter part, he wrote EPHESIANS, COLOSSIANS, PHILEMON, PHILIPPIANS. In A.D. 63 he was released, and remained free until A.D. 67, during which time he visited places in Asia Minor, and Macedonia, and, perhaps, went as far as Spain. Also, during this period he wrote 1 TIMOTHY and TITUS, in A.D. 66–67. In A.D. 68 he was re-arrested, taken to Rome, and there wrote 2 TIMOTHY, A.D. 68, in which year, after two trials, he was murdered, the result of his appeal to Nero.

It is noteworthy that Paul was not put into the prison, and one soldier as guard was thought enough (16, 23, 30). The change in his circumstances is reflected in the *Prison Epistles*. Having ceased to travel, he has more time to think. How fruitful have captivities been ! In addition to these Epistles, we think of the prisoner JOHN, giving us the *Apocalypse*, and the prisoner BUNYAN, giving us the *Pilgrim's Progress*. Are you a captive, bed-ridden, or home-held ? By pen or prayer you may enrich the whole Church of God. We should always endeavour to clear up misunderstandings (17-20), and should always be prepared to confess and defend our faith (21-23). Encouragements and disappointments will follow (24).

Verses 25-29 mark a momentous crisis. Judaism has now fallen ; a long dispensation here ends. It was during this " *two years* " (30) that Onesimus was converted. Times of restraint need not be times of reaction ; we all should always do all the good we can. Paul has done vastly more from his prison for the good of the world than all the Caesars have done from their throne.

Thought : NEVER GIVE UP UNTIL YOU GO UP.